*The Rivers of*
# COSTA RICA

# The Rivers of
# COSTA RICA

## A Canoeing, Kayaking, and Rafting Guide

Michael W. Mayfield and
Rafael E. Gallo

Menasha Ridge Press     Birmingham, Alabama

Published by Menasha Ridge Press
3169 Cahaba Heights Road
Birmingham, AL 35243

First edition, third printing.


**Library of Congress Cataloging-in-Publication Data**
Mayfield, Michael W., 1954–
   The rivers of Costa Rica : a canoeing, kayaking, and rafting guide
   Michael W. Mayfield and Rafael E. Gallo. — 1st ed.
      p.    cm.
   Bibliography: p.
   Includes index.
   ISBN 0-89732-083-2 : $13.95 (est.)
   1. White-water canoeing—Costa Rica—Guide-books.    2. Rafting (Sports)—
Costa Rica—Guide-books.    3. Costa Rica—Description and travel—1981–    —
Guide-books.    I. Gallo, Rafael E., 1958–       II. Title.
GV776.29.C8M39    1988
797.1'22'097286—dc19                                                        88-22783
                                                                                    CIP

Cover photograph of Jim Reid on the Telire River, Costa Rica, by Rafael Gallo.

Cartography by Jeffrey C. Patton, Department of Geography, University of North Carolina at Greensboro.

Book design by Deborah Wong. Cover design by Barbara Williams.

## Dedication

This book is dedicated to the Tenth Street Paddlers: Tom Wise, Kevin Knussmann, Bart Bartram, Brenda Breese, Wade Bullock, Jimmy Nixon, John Dean, Liese Clebsch, Mark Johnson, Mark Hilaridies, Doug McSpadden, and Earl Alderson. Their dedication to the Alfred E. Newman School of Whitewater Thinking made the running of the rivers described herein possible.

# Contents

# List of Maps and Figures

# Acknowledgments

We are deeply indebted to a number of people for the material that appears in this book. Tom Wise, Kevin Knussmann, Brian Wham, and Mary Hipsher contributed their river notes from numerous trips. Kevin also reviewed an early draft of the manuscript and made many helpful remarks and suggestions. Bill Karls and Andy Zimmerman reviewed the book and provided insight on the grading of rapids and rivers. Earl Alderson served as a gung-ho guinea pig for the rapids that we didn't want to try first. We are especially indebted to Fernando Esquivel for his suggestions, encouragement, and enthusiasm, and for keeping the office of Ríos Tropicales in order while Rafael was out on the river. Patty Burkart, Sharon Puryear, Kemp Dalton, Duane Therrialt, and Norman Deal assisted with the cartography. Shirley Brown of the UNCG Geography Department assisted with the typing, much of it from barely legible notes taken at Turrialtico in failing light after long days on the river. LACSA Airlines supported our travels and made it possible for all of us to travel with ease to this tropical utopia.

# Part One: The Country

# An Introduction: The Geography of Costa Rica

The country of Costa Rica is frequently compared to the state of West Virginia and indeed the two have much in common, especially size and abundance of rugged terrain. Yet Costa Rica has three times the rainfall of West Virginia, itself a water-rich domain, and the mountains of Costa Rica reach heights of over 12,000 feet. Even their similarity in size is rather misleading, for the effective size of Costa Rica is far greater than that of its northern sister. As Edward Abbey noted, distance and space

Location of Costa Rica

are functions of speed and time. You can drive from the northern border of West Virginia at Morgantown to Bluefield at its southern border in 5 to 6 hours, but to drive from the Nicaraguan border of Costa Rica to the Panamanian border takes over 15 hours under the best of conditions on the Pan-American Highway. Other routes take considerably longer. The effective size of Costa Rica, then, is far greater than that of a state of similar dimensions in the United States, for vehicles move slowly and time passes deliberately in this vast nation the size of West Virginia. The rugged terrain combined with the drainage network and the great volume of runoff provide more opportunities for whitewater paddling than any other area of comparable dimensions. Surely no other land contains as much paddleable whitewater per square mile as Costa Rica.

# The Climate

December 19, 1985: In Chicago it is −5° F, windy, snowing, and the windchill factor is −21°. Daylight lasts for all of 9 hours; the sun sets at 4:20 P.M. In Pittsburgh it is 1°; it is −15° in Minneapolis. Even in the sunny South, Atlanta has a low temperature of 21° and more of the same is expected for the next three months. Meanwhile, at San Isidro, the put-in for a popular four-to-six-day trip on the Río General, the low is 62°, the high is 84°, skies are brilliantly clear with visibility limited only by towering mountains at all points of the compass, and the day is 12 hours long. The river is sparkling clear as it falls steadily from the thundering chocolate flows of October, and no rain will fall for the next four days. Is there any better reason to travel south for a week, two weeks, or an entire season of paddling in Costa Rica?

Even in the near-equatorial tropics of Costa Rica, which lies between 8° and 11° north latitude, there is considerable variation in weather throughout the year. As the accompanying climate charts show, there is not a great deal of temperature change through the year *at any given location* but the variation *from place to place* is tremendous because of the rugged terrain of this mountain nation. As a general rule, temperatures decline with elevation at a rate of approximately 3.5° per thousand feet in Costa Rica. Thus, the average December temperature in Orotina, at the coast, is 79° F, San José at 3500 feet averages 66° F, while Villa Mills at 10,000 feet averages a chilly 43° F.

San José experiences moderate temperatures throughout the year, with pleasantly warm afternoons and refreshingly cool evenings (see table). Most of the rivers described in this book flow at elevations well below 2,000 feet, where temperatures are ideally suited to paddling. Paddling jackets are sometimes needed to block the sun or for afternoon showers, but wetsuits are never necessary, even on the higher-elevation runs. Many of the rivers in Costa Rica have their headwaters in the high mountain regions of the country, but water temperatures in the high 60s and low 70s will hardly discomfort or disappoint paddlers coming from the North American winter.

**San José Climate**

| Month | Mean Temperature (°F) | Precipitation | |
|---|---|---|---|
| | | Mean, in. | Days with Rain |
| January | 66 | 0.3 | 3 |
| February | 67 | 0.2 | 1 |
| March | 68 | 0.4 | 2 |
| April | 70 | 1.5 | 7 |
| May | 70 | 9.6 | 19 |
| June | 70 | 11.2 | 22 |
| July | 69 | 9.1 | 23 |
| August | 69 | 9.2 | 24 |
| September | 69 | 13.5 | 24 |
| October | 69 | 13.1 | 25 |
| November | 68 | 6.8 | 14 |
| December | 67 | 1.8 | 6 |
| Annual | 69 | 76.7 | 170 |

First-time visitors to Costa Rica often neglect to bring a warm jacket with them after reading about the climates of the coastal regions and the Central Valley. To reach many of the popular rivers from San José, however, it is necessary to drive over one of the major mountain ranges of the country. In driving to the General, for example, one must pass over the 10,000-foot Cerro del Muerte pass, where afternoon temperatures rarely rise above the mid-50s and nighttime temperatures in the 30s are not uncommon. At these upper elevations, cloudy, windy, and cold conditions persist throughout the year.

Seasons in the tropics are marked not by large changes in temperatures but by the rhythmic changes in rainfall that sweep through the equatorial zone. A well-defined double maxima regime of precipitation is common to Central America. In Costa Rica the peak periods of rainfall occur during May to June and September to October, although precipitation remains substantial throughout the period of May to November. September and October are the wettest months of the year, each with over 13 inches of rain at San José and up to twice that amount on some of the eastern slopes of the Central Volcanic Cordillera. February is the driest month of the year, with January and March close behind. The season which the people of Costa Rica call summer (*verano*) is not the high sun period of June to August, but rather, the cooler but fair weather season that the rest of the northern hemisphere calls winter.

Despite the abundance of precipitation during the tropical wet season, the weather is hardly dreary; long periods of rain (*temporales*) are common well to the north in Honduras but are relatively rare in Costa Rica and Panama. Even during the wettest months morning sunshine is abundant, with most rainfall reserved for the afternoon hours on the Pacific slope and the evenings hours on the Caribbean slope. The prodigious rainfall totals are arrived at by remarkably regular rainfall (an average of 25 days in October) rather than by extended periods of rain. This regularity of precipitation provides not only an abundant supply of water to the rivers of the region but a very reliable supply as well; the rivers of Costa Rica flow at seasonal levels that are far more predictable than those of any region of the United States.

Regional variations of precipitation are great within Costa Rica. The lowlands of Guanacaste receive less than 75 inches of rain per year, as does the Central Valley. These areas have extended periods of dry weather from December until April. The wettest areas of Costa Rica are the Caribbean slope, the extreme southern end of Puntarenas, and the windward northeastern slopes of the cordillera. A few mountainous areas receive more than 350 inches of rain per year. None of these areas experience a marked dry season.

From a climatological viewpoint, then, what time of the year is best for a whitewater vacation in Costa Rica? That depends entirely upon the type of water you prefer and the weather you are trying to avoid at home. January, February, and March are the driest and sunniest months of the year in Costa Rica. Rainfall averages only 0.3 inches per month for the three-month period at San José. At the same time, the North American winter is raging full force in the mid-latitudes, making a trip south to the tropics quite appealing. Now for the bad news: River levels drop considerably by late December and most rivers become too low to paddle by mid-January. The Pacuare remains runnable throughout this period, although at very low water levels. The thrilling rapids of Octo-

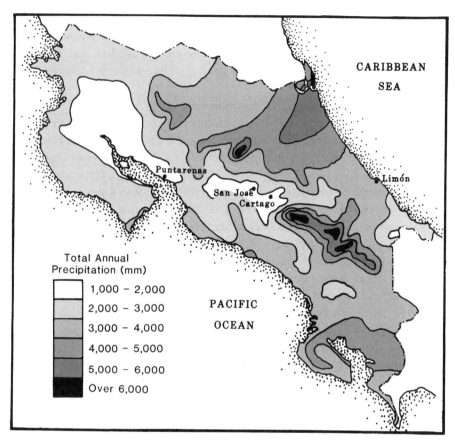

Annual Rainfall in Costa Rica

ber recede drastically, but the Pacuare becomes crystal clear and one has the opportunity to enjoy its beauty and wildlife to a degree not possible when the river is flowing at higher levels. Also, the dam-controlled Reventazón and Corobici remain consistently runnable throughout this period. Fortunately, there are four sections of Class III to V+ white-water on the lower Reventazón alone, so excellent paddling is available even during the dry season. For a tropical vacation combining some paddling on these three rivers with swimming, fishing, surfing, and snorkeling at the beach, this may be the ideal time of year to visit Costa

Rica. As a bonus, the recession of water levels means that normally turbid waters become quite clear during the low-water season. In addition, ocean kayaking is now being offered in the beautiful Gulf of Nicoya and the dry season is the perfect time for ocean touring.

If you prefer the booming high-water conditions that made whirlpool surfing and the 20-foot wave at Chachalaca on the General famous, consider a trip any time during the months of May, June, September, or October. High water levels are almost guaranteed during this period, providing endless surfing opportunities on the General and Sarapiquí, pushy runs on the dry gorge of the Reventazón, and the possibility of sharing in the first descent of one of the region's innumerable unexplored streams.

For intermediate water levels and a somewhat reduced likelihood of

Mary Hipsher surfing Chachalaca, Río General. Photo by Rafael Gallo.

rain, the *veranillo* ("little summer") months of July and August are well suited to those for whom summer months are most opportune for travel. Perhaps the best compromise between high water levels, reduced precipitation rates, and lousy weather back home occurs during the month of November. As can be seen from the individual stream hydrographs, runoff during November is more than adequate for any of the river segments described in this book, while rainfall falls off dramatically in the latter half of the month.

# Hydrology

Costa Rica has an abundance of water. As noted in the previous section, annual rainfall totals reach as high as 350 inches in parts of the country and the Central Valley is considered to be a "dry" area because it receives only seventy to ninety inches of rain per year. The significance of this is not so much that big water is available, but that even small watersheds gather enough runoff to be paddleable. In even the most humid sections of the United States, few watersheds smaller than 150 square miles have enough water in them to kayak for significant portions of the year. The Chattooga River, for example, drains 207 square miles of the wettest area in the eastern United States. Most paddlers consider the Chattooga to be a small river, as its average summer discharge is approximately 400 cfs. The Pacuare River of Costa Rica drains an area of only 142 square miles above the upper put-in but has an average discharge of 1230 cfs. The Peñas Blancas is runnable where the upstream drainage area is a mere 43 square miles. As a result of their heavy runoff loads, small watersheds in Costa Rica produce runnable streams, whereas a watershed of comparable size in the States would yield only a tiny creek.

Of perhaps greater importance to the paddler who goes to considerable trouble and expense in travelling several thousand miles to reach this area is the reliability of stream flows. As the individual stream hydrographs in the following chapters indicate, many of the streams in this region are within the envelope of paddleable flows for much of the year. More importantly, the flows for any particular month of the year are more reliable than those of North America. The reason for this reliability is the fact that the variability of precipitation is quite low throughout the humid tropics. The systems that bring rain in the equatorial zone are quite stable and reliable, unlike the erratic storm systems that move through the mid-latitudes following the fickle jet stream.

While adequate flows are quite reliable, excessive flows can be a problem, especially during September and October. A commercial raft trip from Costa Rica Expeditions was forced to remain in camp for two days of high water on the General in 1984. The members of the group were preparing for an arduous hike out of the canyon when finally the river dropped and they were able to complete their trip. The great variability of flow levels on the General is further exemplified by the flash flood of October 2, 1982, when the river rose more than five feet in less than an hour to reach a discharge level of 26,000 cfs. The river dropped just as quickly to a discharge of less than 10,000 cfs by the following morning.

Also in 1984, a crew was attempting to film a commercial on the Naranjo River for Camel Cigarettes' "rugged outdoors" series when a flash flood roared down the river with a front wave five feet high. The Camel Man was perched midstream on a completely inoperable log raft secured and directed by underwater ropes while he "guided" the raft through a small rapid with the tiller. The surging current snapped the guide ropes instantly, sending Mr. Rugged Outdoors rapidly downstream on an unexplored river. He was quite taken with this new experience, for he had never actually floated down a whitewater river, despite being portrayed as a macho riverman. River guide Tom Wise, who had been hired to provide technical assistance, jumped into his kayak and pursued the runaway raft. Both vessels disappeared around the bend on the swell of the flood. Local newspapers reported the deaths of Messrs. Camel and Wise, but fortunately for all involved, Tom was able to quote Mark Twain in saying that "rumors of my demise have been much exaggerated."

Abundant late-afternoon and early-evening rainstorms frequently cause river levels to rise dramatically during the night, so it is important to carry boats well above the water line when stopping for the night. This should also be considered when choosing a campsite. A new Dancer washed away in the middle of the night on a recent trip down the General, leaving its owners short one boat and turning its American paddler into a raft passenger.

# Natural History

## Geology

The narrow isthmus of Central America stretches from southern Mexico to western Colombia, connecting the continents of North and South America by a tenuous land bridge. This bridge is extremely young in geologic terms, having been formed initially only 11 million years ago. The natural history of Central America has taken place, then, over a period of time equalling only two-tenths of one percent of the earth's age.

The gross features of Central American geology are best understood through the plate tectonic model. The earth's uppermost layer is divided into numerous brittle plates which slide across the more flexible layer beneath, so that there is substantial relative motion between adjacent plates. The driving force behind this motion is sea-floor spreading at the mid-ocean ridges. At these ridges, fresh crustal material is constantly being generated. The new rock wedges the adjacent plates apart, moving them in opposite directions at a rate of one to four inches per year. Where an oceanic plate collides with a continental plate, the oceanic plate is subducted beneath the continental plate, accompanied by crumpling of the crust, earthquakes, and volcanic intrusions from melting of the subducted plate.

Costa Rica lies on the leading edge of the Caribbean plate, where it is colliding with the Cocos plate. The Cocos plate is being driven under the Caribbean plate by spreading at the Galapagos Rift Zone. As a result, Central America is being built by folding of the edge of the Caribbean plate (like a rug pushed into a wall) and by magma surging upward to form the volcanic ranges that form the backbone of the isthmus. The subduction process is not a smooth one; the Cocos plate snags and breaks loose intermittently, producing earthquakes such as the one that destroyed much of Cartago in 1910. The continuing volcanic activity at Poás, Arenal, Irazú, and Rincón de la Vieja is forceful evidence of the continuation of this process.

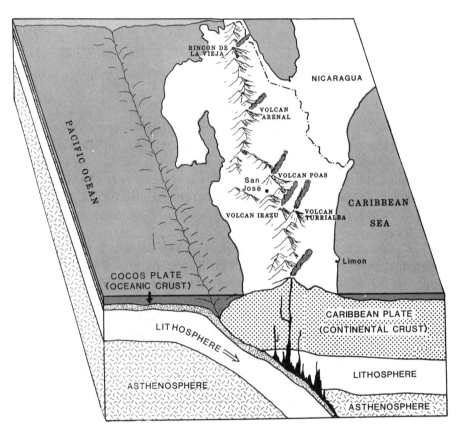

Geologic Cross-section of Costa Rica

## Landform Regions of Costa Rica

Costa Rica is a land dominated by mountains and isolated, undeveloped coasts. The Caribbean coast is constantly pounded by waves generated by the ceaseless Trade Winds, producing some of the world's best surf (which goes largely unnoticed by the surfing community). Beaches of brilliant white and improbably rich black sand reach, in many segments, twenty to forty miles at a clip without a single seawall, groin, jetty, revetment, or condominium. The primary residents of parts of the

Caribbean zone are sea turtles, which lay their massive eggs on the beaches, and the equally laid-back Rastafarians who derive a meager financial income from catching lobsters and a rich psychic income from this beautiful environment. At Cahuita, a national park preserves the only coral reef in Costa Rica. Fine beaches, lush forests, and spectacular marine life are the main attractions here.

The Pacific coast is quite different from the Caribbean coast in nearly every respect. The length of the Pacific coastline is over twice that of the Atlantic coast due to the nature of the borders and the presence of two

large peninsulas, Nicoya and Osa. The Pacific coast has a much drier climate than the Caribbean and this is reflected in the forms of natural vegetation and in the agricultural landscape. Guanacaste, the north-western province of Costa Rica, has been largely converted to cattle ranching. Expansive haciendas are the most common farm type here, with most of these operations covering over 500 acres and some approaching 10,000 acres. This is in great contrast to the central valley, where small family farms are most common. The cattle ranches are famous for the modern-day cowboys who ride the range in attire borrowed from their Texas heroes.

Many of the Pacific beaches are quite remote, with little access by road. The tidal range here is up to 12 feet, as compared to only 1 to 2 feet on the Caribbean coast, and there are many places with excellent surf. One of the most visited beaches is at Quepos, where part of the coast has been preserved as Manuel Antonio National Park. Daily flights from San José provide easy access to this area for a fare of only about $15.00.

Four major mountain ranges form the backbone of this narrow isthmus connecting the Americas. Three of them consist of young volcanic material, two with actively erupting peaks, but each has its own unique character. There are substantial differences in the length, breadth, and heights of the peaks as well as large differences in climate and ecological communities established on each range.

Stretching from Lake Nicaragua southeastward for some 65 miles is the Cordillera de Guanacaste, which is only slightly higher than 6000 feet at its crest, but it is quite rugged, consisting of active and recently active volcanoes. The Arenal volcano has been known to erupt violently, as in 1968 when a nuee ardente (a dense cloud of ash and hot gases) roared down its slopes, with temperatures of over 600° C. It was just this type of eruption of Mt. Pelee that destroyed St. Pierre, Martinique, and its 28,000 residents in 1902. Fortunately, this area of Costa Rica is, for the most part, sparsely populated; only 68 people died in the 1968 eruption. That eruption episode emitted over 10 million cubic meters of lava and an equal amount of airborne ash and cinders. In 1985 two American kayakers were hiking up the steep upper slopes when the cone began to spew out gravel-size particles of debris, forcing them to retreat hastily downslope. Another active volcano in the chain, Rincón de la Vieja, has been protected as a national park. The Cordillera de Guanacaste is separated from the other mountains to the southeast by a rift that has filled with water to form Lake Arenal. Of the many rivers draining this chain of mountains, only the Corobici and Tempisque have been paddled because roads are scarce in the area, making access very difficult.

The Cordillera de Tilarán is an older group of volcanic mountains of slightly greater width but lesser height than the Cordillera de Guanacaste. No roads penetrate the interior of the range. Because of the lack of access, only the Río Penas Blancas, Toro, and Tres Amigos have been explored by boat. Other streams draining the Cordillera de Tilarán that show promise for future exploration include the Cañas and Lagarto. None of the volcanoes of the Tilarán range are active.

Far taller than the two previous mountain ranges stands the massive Cordillera Central, formed of two active and two potentially active volcanoes and their subsidiary flanks. Poás Volcano has numerous craters near its 8870-foot summit which contain boiling mud pots, fumaroles, and the tallest geyser in the world. Poás has undergone at least seven eruptive sequences since the turn of the century, most recently in 1980. The cities of Alajuela and San José are intermittently dusted with volcanic ash from those eruptions.

Irazú Volcano towers over the Central Valley, with its broad-based peak reaching an elevation of 11,257 feet. The colonial capital of Cartago lies on its southern flank and, together with Turrialba, its twin peak, Irazú forms the northwestern flank of the Reventazón valley. During an eruptive phase that lasted from 1963 to 1965, over 100 square kilometers of the surrounding land were devastated. Material erupted from the summit and filled the channel of the Reventado River, forcing a change in the course of the river and flooding riverside communities. A paved road leads to the summit from Cartago, providing fascinating views of the smoldering craters and the best land-based perspective of the region that is available. Eruptions of Poás and Irazú have provided the rich volcanic soils upon which much of the country's coffee crop grows, but future eruptions pose a serious environmental hazard to the populations of the nearby cities.

Sheltered from the rain-bearing trade winds by the towering peaks of the Cordillera Central is the Central Valley. Two-thirds of all Costa Ricans live in this upland basin, at altitudes that fall between 2000 and 4900 feet. Lying in the rain shadow of the high peaks, San José receives only one-third the rainfall that soaks the northeast slopes of the Cordillera Central, and the high elevations of the Central Valley ensure mild temperatures throughout the year. A maze of streams drains the area, joining to form the raging Río Grande de Tárcoles. Unfortunately, the raw sewage effluent from nearly a million people and their industries ends up in the Virilla, Tirribi, Tuís, and Grande de Tárcoles, rendering them entirely unpaddleable.

By far the largest of the mountain ranges in Costa Rica is the Cordillera de Talamanca, a massive non-volcanic range which stretches from Cartago southeastward into Panama. Included in the range is Cerro Chirripó, which reaches 12,529 feet above sea level. The Pan-American Highway climbs over the Cordillera de Talamanca as it heads south from Cartago, gaining an elevation of over 10,000 feet as it passes over Cerro la Muerte ("Mountain of Death"). On a clear day both the Pacific Ocean and Caribbean Sea are visible from this stretch of highway. Orographic uplift of moisture-laden trade winds produces the rainfall which flows off this massif to form the Reventazón, Pacuare, Chirripó, Telire, General, and scores of other rivers.

Between the Talamancas and the low Pacific coastal ranges is a broad depression known as the General/Coto Brus Valley, or the Térraba Trough. See the chapter on the General watershed for more information on this scenic valley, which is ripe with whitewater rivers. The remaining Pacific lowland area is quite narrow except to the far northwest, where the rolling Nicoya Peninsula reaches over 50 miles toward the Pacific from the Cordillera de Guanacaste.

The Caribbean lowlands comprise extensive areas to the northeast of the country's mountain backbone. Along the foothills of the mountains are many farms and small villages, but the true lowlands are quite sparsely populated. In the extreme northeast area no roads penetrate the fecund jungle and the only settlements are along navigable rivers such as the San Carlos and lower Sarapiquí. The central portion of Limón has been largely settled and converted into agricultural lands. This settle-

Huacas Falls, Río Pacuare. Photo by Rafael Gallo.

ment was largely the result of the accessibility that the area enjoys, first provided by the Atlantic railroad line and subsequently reinforced by the development of the road from Limón to San José.

Access is also limited and settlements sparse in the southeastern Valle de Talamanca and Valle de la Estrella. This land is largely in the control of several Indian tribes, including the Bribri and Cabecar. A rich network of rivers descends from the lofty heights of the Talamanca Range. The Uren, Telire, Lari, Estrella and Coen join near Suretka to form the Sixaola, a stream of great importance to the banana trade. This great river has been used for many years as a liquid highway for the plantations. Of this great wealth of rivers, only relatively short sections of the Telire and Estrella have been paddled. The others show great promise but the lack of accessibility has frustrated attempts thus far.

# The People of Costa Rica

Costa Rica has a population of over 2.5 million people, and, as the accompanying map indicates, they are heavily concentrated in the Central Valley. One-half of the population lives in this small area, which represents only five percent of the country's land area. Nearly one-half of the population is considered to live in urban locations, a very high percentage for third world countries as a whole. The population growth rate is relatively high; if it continues at the present rate, the population

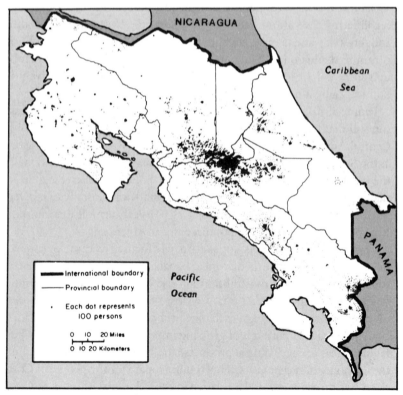

Population Distribution of Costa Rica

will double in about 25 years. This population pressure is one of the reasons why deforestation of the forests of Central America is occurring at a rapid pace.

Costa Rica possesses a uniformity in ethnicity and culture that is not matched anywhere else in Latin America. The vast majority (95 percent) of its population is of Spanish descent, speaks Spanish as the primary language, and adheres to Roman Catholicism. The remaining 5 percent is evenly divided between English-speaking blacks of West Indian origin and native Indians, most of whom live in isolated enclaves throughout the country.

Because large-scale plantation agriculture never dominated the economy of this nation as it did throughout the rest of the region, the basic social institutions were never dominated by a social and economic elite. Small farms have always been at the core of the Costa Rican economy and lifestyle, and a resolute independence and democratic tradition continue to this day. The country has a long tradition of democracy, unlike its neighbors, and nearly every citizen participates actively in political campaigns and elections.

People unfamiliar with the region often assume that the political turmoil that has troubled Nicaragua and El Salvador is typical of all of Central America, but this is far from true. Costa Rica is often described as the Switzerland of the Americas, and the analogy has more to do with the stable democratic government and its policy of relative neutrality than it does with the size and terrain of Costa Rica. Costa Rica is a very safe place to travel, in that there is less political turmoil than in most European countries and the populace is pro-American.

Costa Rica's economy is not as narrowly focused as those of some of its neighbors, but exports of coffee, bananas, sugar, and other agricultural products are the most important part of the economy. Tourism is of increasing importance; it is now a close second to agricultural exports in the generation of foreign exchange in the nation's economy. In addition, light manufacturing is of growing importance. High energy prices, falling prices for agricultural products, and high interest rates have hurt the economy in recent years. This is unfortunate for the people of Costa Rica, but the stronger dollar relative to the colon makes travel to Costa Rica even cheaper for foreigners.

Education and public health are high-priority items in Costa Rica. As a result, the literacy rate is quite high and infectious diseases have been largely eradicated in even the most rural parts of the country. Costa Rica has no army, but does maintain a small national guard unit. Expenditures for national security amount to only 2.6 percent of the national budget, one-tenth of what is spent by the central government on education.

# Travel in Costa Rica

## Getting There

Although it is possible to reach Costa Rica by driving down the Pan American Highway via Mexico, Guatemala, El Salvador, Honduras, and Nicaragua, the present political situation in Nicaragua and El Salvador makes this mode of travel unattractive. The only reasonable alternative is to fly. In addition to the regional carriers, several U.S. airlines, including American and United, fly to San Jose from Miami, New Orleans, and Los Angeles. LACSA, the national airline of Costa Rica, also provides international service via those cities. Connections can be made with ease through those cities from any point in North America. Fares are quite reasonable, with the best prices running during the low tourist season, generally from April through mid-November. The outfitters listed in the next section can provide convenient itineraries and attractive fares.

In order to enter Costa Rica, you will need a passport, but U.S. and Canadian citizens do not need a visa. For visits longer than 30 days, you will need to contact the Costa Rican consulate in advance of your travel. A tourist card is issued for a nominal fee (presently $3 U.S.) at airports serving San José. In addition, a nominal exit tax is levied upon departure.

Most visitors to Costa Rica go there without acquiring any immunizations or medication, but it would be wise to check with your personal physician for individual recommendations. Some prefer for their patients to obtain typhoid immunizations, and people who plan to visit coastal areas are advised to take malaria pills. Up-to-date recommendations on such cautionary procedures are issued by the Public Health Service.

# Getting Around

People who speak Spanish fluently, have plenty of time and money to spend, have detailed topographic maps that they can interpret with the skill of a cartographer, are expert paddlers capable of unaided descents of unknown rivers, and who have the mettle and chutzpah to drive in Central America, might want to consider going to Costa Rica on their own—all others should hire a guide for at least their first trip. While pidgin Spanish and gestures will suffice in San José and the coastal resorts, one could hardly expect to gather directions to a put-in from a *campesino* in rural Guanacaste or San Carlos without command of the language. Detailed topographic maps are crucial for ascertaining correct turns from landforms; signs and word of mouth are not adequate because there are many villages that go by similar or even identical names. There are at least two villages named Bajo Pacuare on the Pacuare River, for example. Most road maps of Central America are woefully incomplete and road markings are only occasionally provided. Because of these problems, an American raft group put in on the Class V–VI upper Pacuare in 1984 thinking that they were starting down the Class III (IV) lower Pacuare. The results could have been disastrous.

A lot of time will be needed for unaided trips because even anyone described above will make many wrong turns and shuttles will prove to be almost impossible. A thick wallet will be needed to pay for rental vehicle(s). Costa Rica imposes an import duty on automobiles of approximately 200 percent, which the rental company must pass along to you. The local rent-a-car agencies are notorious for their add-on charges. We were recently charged $500 for minor roof damage caused by our racks and the rubbing of boats on the roof of our rented van. Rush-hour traffic in San José has been described as "a bullfight on the streets, with every car a blaring beast." Mountain driving is even more exciting, as trucks and buses blithely pass one another on blind curves. Finding one's way through San José or Cartago is nearly impossible because routes are not well marked and drivers generally ignore traffic signs. The old line—"driving to the river is more dangerous than kayaking"—that you've been telling to worrisome parents, friends, and spouses over the years takes on new meaning and validity in Latin America. We won't even discuss the difficulties of getting boats from the United States to Costa Rica.

It is simpler, safer, cheaper, and far easier to take a rafting or kayaking tour with a licensed Costa Rican outfitter. They have top-of-the-line boats and equipment and, more importantly, the experience and expertise to provide a great river trip. Regular package tours are available, but the operators are more than willing to custom design a trip on any river or rivers that you desire. For a very reasonable price they will provide equipment, guides, shuttles, and superb food. Write or call directly to the addresses below for information, or see your favorite raft company—most of them operate trips for their customers through the Costa Rican companies.

Rios Tropicales, S.A.
P.O. Box 472-1200
Pavas, Costa Rica
Phone: (506) 33-6455
FAX (506) 55-4354

Rios Tropicales maintains a full fleet of modern whitewater boats, including Perception Dancers and Corsicas, Dagger Crossfires, open canoes, slalom racers, and squirt boats. They have a wide variety of rafts, including self-bailers for some of the more difficult rivers.

Costa Rica Expeditions
P.O. Box 6941
San José, Costa Rica
Phone: (506) 57-0766
FAX (506) 57-1665

### American Outfitters That Offer Costa Rica Trips:

Nantahala Outdoor Center
U.S. 19W, Box 41
Bryson City, North Carolina 28713
(704) 488-2175

NOC offers trips for intermediate and expert paddlers on the General, Pacuare, and Reventazon. More difficult trips are available on request.

Middle Fork River Company
P.O. Box 54
Sun Valley, ID 83353
Phone (208) 726-8888
FAX (208) 726-2288

Middle Fork River Company offers a full line of Costa Rica river tours, including all of the sections of the Reventazón, Pacuare, Sarapiqui, and the General.

Sobek-Mountain Travel
6420 Fairmont Ave.
El Cerrito, CA 94530
Phone (800) 227-2384
FAX (510) 525-7710

Sobek will customize itineraries for small groups or individuals, which include rafting, beaches, and national parks.

Madawaska Kanu Centre
39 First Ave.
Ottawa, ON, CANADA K1S 2G1
(613) 756-3620 summer      (613) 594-KANU winter

Madawaska offers intermediate and expert kayaking and rafting trips on all the rivers described in this book.

Arizona Raft Adventures
4050-Z E. Huntington Dr.
Flagstaff, AZ 86004
(800) 786-RAFT      (602) 526-8200

AzRA offers raft trips on the Reventazón and Pacuare, including the Class V Peralta section of the Reventazón. Trips depart every month of the year.

The following outfitters offer all of the standard river tours, plus customized itineraries for national park visits and more.

Mariah Expeditions
P.O. Box 248
Point Richmond, CA 94807
(510) 233-2303
FAX (510) 233-0956

Project RAFT
2855 Telegraph Ave.
Suite 309
Berkeley, CA 94705
Phone (415) 704-8222
FAX (415) 704-8322

Journeys
904 West Highland Dr.
Seattle, WA 98119
(206) 284-8890
(800) 345-HIKE

Baja Expeditions (sea kayak tours)
2625 Garnet Ave.
San Diego, CA 92109
(619) 581-3311

Eurotrek
MalzsTrasse 17-21
Postfach
GH 8036
Zurich, SWITZERLAND

# Part Two: The Rivers

# Rating the Difficulty of the Rivers

There is nothing in the sport of whitewater boating that is as controversial as river difficulty ratings. No matter what rating system is used, the assignment of a difficulty rating to an individual rapid or an entire river comes down to the subjective judgement of the individual who is rating the river. The judgement of the individual making such a decision will be affected by his or her paddling skills, preferred river types, experience, and past successes or failures on that stretch of river.

Many proposals have been made for adjusting, upgrading, or entirely replacing the old standard scale, the American Whitewater Affiliation's International Scale of River Difficulty. While some of these proposals have considerable merit, no consensus has been reached within the whitewater community about adopting a new scale or standard for reference. Therefore, we will begin with the AWA scale:

Class I. | Moving water with a few riffles and small waves. Few or no obstructions.

Class II. | Easy rapids with waves up to three feet, and wide, clear channels that are obvious without scouting. Some maneuvering is required.

Class III. | Rapids with high, irregular waves often capable of swamping an open canoe. Narrow passages that often require complex maneuvering. May require scouting from shore.

Class IV. | Long, difficult rapids with constricted passages that often require precise maneuvering in very turbulent waters. Scouting from shore is often necessary, and conditions make rescue difficult. Generally not possible for open canoes. Boaters in covered canoes and kayaks should be able to Eskimo roll.

Class V. | Extremely difficult, long, and very violent rapids with highly congested routes that nearly always must be scouted from shore. Rescue conditions are difficult and there is significant hazard to life in event of a mishap. Ability to Eskimo roll is essential for kayaks and canoes.

Class VI.    Difficulties of Class V carried to the extreme of navigability. Nearly impossible and very dangerous. For teams of experts only, after close study and with all precautions taken.

As a caveat to the above system, the AWA suggests that "if rapids on a river generally fit into one of the following classifications, but the water temperature is below 50 degrees F, or if the trip is an extended trip in a wilderness area, the river should be considered one class more difficult than normal." While cold water is never a problem in Costa Rica, isolation is the rule rather than the exception. Even when roads and towns are nearby, help is not.

There are no organized rescue squads in Costa Rica. Adequate medical facilities for treatment of difficulties as simple as a broken leg are available only in the larger cities, which are several hours away from most of the river sections described here. The language barrier is never more difficult than in a medical emergency. The gestures and 20-word Spanish vocabulary that are adequate for ordering a meal or for finding general directions are of little use in such a situation. As a minimum, any group travelling alone in Costa Rica should have a complete first-aid kit and at least one person with advanced first-aid training. The commercial operators always have trained individuals and very complete first-aid kits which include antivenom for poisonous snakes such as the deadly fer-de-lance.

There are certainly problems associated with applying the AWA scale to unfamiliar rivers. To a person who is quite comfortable paddling Class IV+ big water, an initial trip on a small, technical Class III stream can be quite uncomfortable, and the same can be said for a creek paddler thrown into big water for the first time. For this reason, we have attempted to describe the essential character of each river as well as provide a rating.

Great discrepancies exist in the rating of rivers not only on an individual basis, but on a regional basis as well. Much has been written on the differences in ratings found in the Eastern United States versus the West. As a means of bridging this gap, we have listed below many of the popular whitewater rivers of various portions of the United States by our interpretation of the AWA scale and our subjective judgement:

| | |
|---|---|
| Class II: | Nantahala, N.C. |
| | Grande Ronde, Wash.-Oreg. |
| | Willamette, Oreg. (through Eugene) |
| Class III: | Arkansas (Brown's Canyon), Colo. |
| | Nolichucky (below 2.7′), N.C. |
| | Chattooga (Section III), S.C. |
| | Clackamas, Oreg. |
| | Deschutes, Oreg. |
| | Ocoee, Tenn. |
| Class IV: | New (up to 4′), W. Va. |
| | Lochsa, Idaho |
| | Hells Canyon, Oreg.-Idaho |
| | Arkansas (The Numbers at 2.5′), Colo. |
| | Chattooga (Section IV to 2.1′), S.C.-Ga. |
| Class V: | Gauley, W. Va. |
| | Watauga, N.C. |
| | Arkansas (Pine Creek Canyon), Colo. |
| | Cherry Creek (with portages), Calif. |
| | Colorado (Gore Canyon), Colo. |

Note that we have rated rivers rather than individual rapids. Individual drops on some of the rivers listed above are one grade higher in difficulty than the river as a whole. For example, Bull Sluice on Section III of the Chattooga is a solid Class IV even at low water. In the river descriptions we note such exceptions, and in the river data headings a river with a general rating of Class III with an individual rapid of Class IV would be listed as Class III (IV). All of these ratings reflect our best judgement of a river's difficulty at moderate water levels. Most rivers are more difficult and dangerous at higher water levels. In addition, tropical rivers are subject to substantial modification by flash floods. The fluvial system of Costa Rica is a very volatile one due to the intensity of precipitation and the steepness of upper slopes. For example, heavy rains falling on the eastern slopes of the Cordillera Central in early July of 1987 caused heavy flooding of the upper tributaries of the Reventazón. As a result, the channels of the Pejibaye and Atirro rivers were heavily scoured and numerous logjams were left behind as the floodwaters receded. Sections of the Pejibaye that are ordinarily simple Class II beginner's runs became so choked with debris as to be temporarily unrunnable. A tremendous flood occurred on the Pacuare in December 1987 which altered most of the major rapids, making many of them more congested and more difficult to run. Fortunately, an even higher flood occurred two weeks later which scoured out the channel, making

Río Pacuare: Upper Huacas Rapid. Photo by Rafael Gallo.

the rapids even better than before the first flood. Due to the frequency of flooding in the tropics, change is the only thing that remains constant about these rivers. We believe these ratings and descriptions to be accurate as of mid-1988, but caution is advised, as rapids may have changed since the book went to press.

# Using This Guidebook

For the many reasons listed above, paddling new rivers in Costa Rica is far more difficult than it is in the States. No guidebook, including this one, can provide a thorough enough description of any river to make an unaided trip safe by North American standards. We have not tried to explain how to run the rapids, but rather to describe the general characteristics of the rivers and their relative difficulties. To a degree unmatched in any other part of the world, tropical river systems are hydrologically and geomorphically unstable. Rainfall arrives in copious amounts here, allowing rivers to rise rapidly. River channels are frequently altered by floods and flotsam, so the character and degree of difficulty of the individual rapids are subject to change. There are simply no substitutes for experience, individual judgement, and careful examination of river conditions.

In the individual river profiles, we have tried to provide the information most needed by paddlers. The degree of difficulty assigned to each river is obviously a subjective decision; we have listed our criteria and standards of reference in the section above.

River gradients were measured from 1:50,000-scale topographic maps and converted from metric to English units. Rounding of values has resulted in minor discrepancies as compared to the listed elevations and length of the river segment. Where parts of the river have substantially higher gradients than the section as a whole, we list partial gradients. For example, the upper Pacuare is listed as "76 feet per mile (three @ 94 feet per mile)." This means that the average gradient of the entire section is 76 feet per mile, but a three-mile stretch drops at a rate of 94 feet per mile.

The listed length of each section was also determined from 1:50,000 maps and rounded to the nearest tenth of a mile. Rivers that frequently split into multiple channels, such as the lower Peñas Blancas, could be several tenths of a mile longer, depending on which channels you choose to take.

Elevations listed for the put-ins and take-outs are accurate to the nearest ten meters, as determined from the available topographic maps. This information can be quite useful in cross-checking information listed here against topographic maps in the event that there is any confusion about specific access points.

In most cases, the drainage areas listed in each river heading were obtained from the Costa Rican hydrologic survey office at Instituto Costarricense de Electricidad (ICE). Drainage areas of ungaged streams were measured from topographic maps. The size of the drainage area above a given river reach will usually reveal a lot of information about the character of the river and the duration of high and low flows. Rivers with a drainage area of less than 200 square miles are usually quite small and technical and tend to have rapid runoff. As the drainage area grows

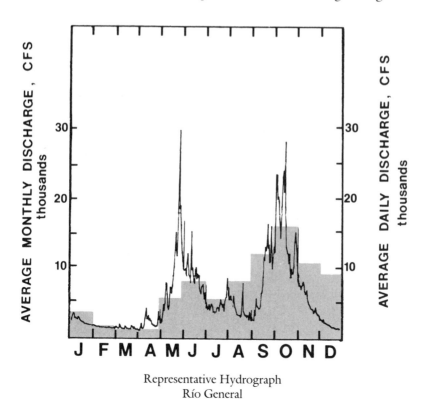

Representative Hydrograph
Río General

larger, the dependability of flow increases as the extremes of flow decrease. In addition, these larger streams such as the General and Reventazón tend to have more open rapids than the smaller creeks.

Average discharge values reinforce what the drainage area values suggest, but these yearly averages can be misleading due to great seasonal variations. For this reason, we have provided representative hydrographs for all streams for which the necessary information is available. On each of these hydrographs, the average monthly discharge is shown as a bar graph in the background and the average daily discharge for a single representative year is shown as a bold, irregular curve. Monthly averages are indicative of typical conditions for each month, while the daily values for a single year reveal the characteristic fluctuations that are likely to occur on a short-term basis. In the example below, one can see that the General has its highest monthly discharge of 7000 cfs in October, while occasional peaks of 30,000 cfs are not uncommon. The paddling season listed is based on average or typical conditions, although occasional heavy rains will make any of the rivers paddleable for a day or two at a time even during its normally dry season. Conversely, occasional dry periods may render streams unpaddleable even during the peak wet season. Such occurrences are rare, however, and the dam-controlled Reventazón always has enough water for paddling.

# Río Sarapiquí

The lower Sarapiquí (sae ruh puh KEE) River is an excellent choice for a first day trip upon arriving in Costa Rica. The scenery is spectacular, the rapids are moderate, and the wildlife would have any Audubon Society member babbling ecstatically. The upper section of the river, with a gradient of 90 feet per mile and tight boulder-laden drops, provides all of the scenic attractions of the lower section, with expert-level paddling as well.

For the travel-weary new arrival to the tropics, the drive from San José through the Central Volcanic Cordillera to the valley of the Sarapiquí delivers a stunning, invigorating introduction to the verdant tropical rain forest. While much of that dense virgin forest has been cleared for agriculture, the complex patterns of tropical agriculture result in a cultural landscape of refreshing diversity. Surrounding the route are dense fields of bananas, coffee, strawberries, papayas, and ferns. In climbing over the southeast shoulder of the immense Poás Volcano, one climbs into the cool, perpetually wet cloud forest and larger remnants of the natural vegetation complex are encountered. Dense stands of forest shroud the windward slopes of the volcano as the road descends the eastern side of the Cordillera. This side of the range faces the full force of the nearly perennial trade winds, wringing copious amounts of rainfall from the moisture-laden air as it is forced to ascend the 10,000-foot summits. The prodigious rainfall supports untold numbers of headwater streams, which cascade off the volcanic cone to form the Sarapiquí River. Several of these waterfalls are visible from the highway, including La Paz ("Peace") falls, which are adjacent to the highway and easily accessible. A short side road leads to a spectacular pair of waterfalls, El Congo and Salto del Angel, which plunge 500 feet into a clear pool. The abundant water also supports rich vegetation forms such as the "Poor Man's Umbrella," with thick waxy leaves up to six feet in diameter. Anyone caught without shelter during a typical afternoon torrent comes quickly to an appreciation of the practicality of this unusual plant.

## Río Sarapiquí

**Section:** San Miguel to La Virgen
**Degree of Difficulty:** Class IV, V
**Gradient:** 90 feet per mile
**Length:** 6.9 miles
**Put-in Elevation:** 1180 feet
**Take-out Elevation:** 560 feet
**Drainage Area:** Approximately 125 square miles
**Average Discharge:** Approximately 1000 cfs
**Season:** June through December

Eastern creek paddlers will feel right at home on the upper Sarapiquí, as it is quite steep and each rapid is extremely congested with boulders. Although boat scouting will suffice for paddlers with the necessary skills to run this stretch of water, rapid, decisive moves are required in order to avoid pins. The first rapid, which can be easily scouted from the bridge at the put-in, is typical of the drops to be found throughout this section. The character of this rapid is easily seen from this convenient vantage point, but the height of the bridge makes it difficult to appreciate the magnitude of the drop itself. Paddlers must watch constantly for strainers in this section, for the river is extremely narrow and trees hang across it for extended stretches. Frequent evening flashfloods from heavy rains in the mountains constantly alter the rapids and sometimes lodge trees between the large boulders that choke the channel, so watch carefully for strainers.

Named rapids in this section include the Banana, The Mush, and Me Gusta ("I like it"). The Banana is a steep rapid that has a banana-shaped vertical drop at the exit. The Mush has a six-foot waterfall at its terminus which pours into an aerated hole. Obscured from above by a house-sized boulder, Me Gusta appears unrunnable at first. The entire flow of the river rushes against the boulder, forming a powerful pillow on the upstream side, with clean four-foot drops on each side.

It would be very difficult to hike out from this section because it has very dense forest alongside it and the valley walls are quite steep. Pins are a constant concern and when the flow is high enough to pad all of

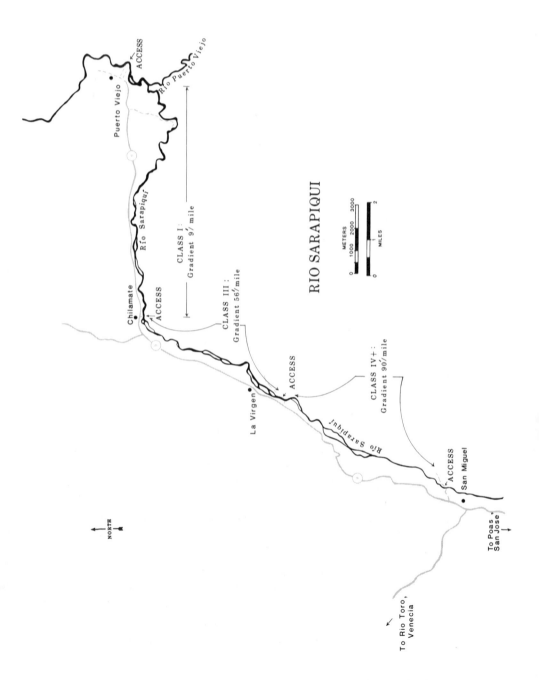

RIO SARAPIQUI

CLASS I:
Gradient 9'/mile

CLASS III:
Gradient 56'/mile

CLASS IV+:
Gradient 90'/mile

ACCESS

ACCESS

ACCESS

ACCESS

ACCESS

Puerto Viejo

Río Puerto Viejo

Río Sarapiquí

Chilamate

La Virgen

Río Sarapiquí

San Miguel

To Poas,
San Jose

To Río Toro,
Venecia

NORTH

METERS
0   1000  2000  3000
MILES
0        1        2

Río Sarapiquí   41

the rocks, the holes get grabby. We recommend paddling it at relatively low water (800-1500 cfs) in plastic boats. This is no place for rafts.

Fernando Esquivel and Rafael Gallo attempted to run the upper Sarapiquí in 1984 in a two-man raft, but the raft was damaged by the continuous rocky rapids and the pair had to abandon the run two miles above La Virgen. The first complete descent was accomplished in kayaks the following year by Joe Pulliam, Rafael Gallo, and a group of paddlers from Atlanta.


## Río Sarapiquí

**Section: La Virgen to Chilamate**
**Degree of Difficulty:** Class III
**Gradient:** 56 feet per mile
**Length:** 7.0 miles
**Put-in Elevation:** 558 feet
**Take-out Elevation:** 164 feet
**Drainage Area:** Approximately 150 square miles
**Average Discharge:** 2200 cfs
**Season:** June through December


From the put-in below the bridge at La Virgen to the take-out at Chilamate the Sarapiquí courses through lush Atlantic Coast rainforest and beautifully manicured fields of sugar cane, bananas, oil palm, and cacao while dropping over innumerable gravel bar rapids. Most of the rapids are quite simple and are easily boat scouted, but many of them follow a somewhat disconcerting tendency to terminate in a direct shot into vertical walls of naturally cemented boulder terraces. On these rapids, it is necessary to cut diagonally across the current to avoid hitting the embankment.

The first rapid of note, Hueco Gringo ("Gringo's Hole"), is a long, straight rapid that ends in a nice hole at bottom center. The rapid becomes progressively steeper as you descend it. Another memorable drop follows. Beginning in much the same fashion as Hueco Gringo, its terminus is quite different. Instead of terminating against a wall, it

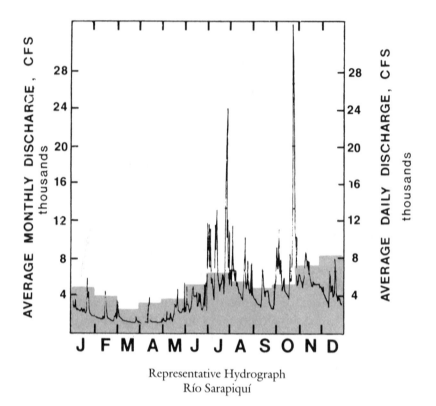

Representative Hydrograph
Río Sarapiquí

suddenly enters a complex boulder garden which has at least four possible routes. The rapid is known as Confusion. Just another quarter mile downstream is a dangerous rapid, Pattie's Bend. It is found approximately four miles down the river. Looking no different from any of the other boulder gardens, this rapid sweeps left to right over a series of drops which end in a strainer where the main current passes through a group of robust tree roots on the left bank. Paddle rafts in particular have difficulty in avoiding this hazard, so it is important to recognize this rapid before entering it and to begin a left-to-right ferry as soon as possible.

Bird watchers will have a field day on the Sarapiquí, as groups of toucans, parrots, bitterns, herons, hawks, oro pendulas ("gold tails"), and huge kingfishers fly busily throughout the river corridor. In many places the river splits into multiple intimate channels where huge trees draped with epiphytes and orchids hang directly over the water. This is indeed the tropics!

The take-out is at a small bar and restaurant on the left bank of the river where drinks and food may be obtained at a very reasonable price—not a bad ending to an unbelievable river trip. Great care should be taken at the take-out, as a fallen tree has created a dangerous strainer just past the restaurant. An ill-advised swim here resulted in a near fatality following a raft trip in 1986. The shuttle ride back to the put-in is short and direct, as the road follows the river closely, but remains unseen from the river.

The lower Sarapiquí was first paddled in December 1984 by kayakers Jon Sheppard, Andy Zimmerman, Jim Reed, Rafael Gallo, Tom Wise, and Earl Alderson. Although the group was mildly disappointed by the lack of difficult whitewater, they were immensely impressed by the scenery. Commercial raft trips were soon begun on the lower river by Rios Tropicales and this section is now one of the most popular one-day raft trips in Costa Rica due to its magnificent wildlife and fun rapids.

## Río Sarapiquí

**Section: Chilamate to Puerto Viejo**
**Degree of Difficulty:** Class I
**Gradient:** 9.0 feet per mile
**Length:** 7.3 miles
**Put-in Elevation:** 164 feet
**Take-out Elevation:** 98 feet
**Drainage Area:** 317 square miles
**Average Discharge:** 4400 cfs
**Season:** June through January

This section contains nothing but flatwater, but the scenery is still pretty enough to justify paddling it. All of the wildlife found on the section above is found in greater concentrations on this lower section, but one is also likely to see monkeys, mot-mot birds, and other wildlife that avoids the farmlands of the upper section. Small commercial craft ply the river from the Caribbean to Puerto Viejo via the San Juan River, a distance of over 50 miles. It is not unusual to see dugout canoes on the river below Chilamate.

One of the most unusual characteristics of the Caribbean slope streams is their sudden change of slope. On the Sarapiquí, the gradient drops from 45 feet per mile to less than 10 feet per mile in less than a mile, with the change occurring at Chilamate. The Toro and Tres Amigos undergo similar changes in slope.

# Río General System

Including the largest whitewater river in Costa Rica, the General (HEN uh RAL) watershed contains over 100 miles of paddleable streams. Within the valley of the General are marginally runnable creeks with gradients in excess of 200 feet per mile, intermediate river segments known primarily for their scenery and wildlife, and gentle segments suitable for beginners. The General is known worldwide for a different type of whitewater, however. It is the huge rapids ideally suited for surfing that have gained international renown for this river more than any other aspect: complex rapids such as Chirripó Grande and brutally simple rapids such as Chachalaca. Play spots are innumerable, including ender holes, side-surfing holes, big waves, and every possible hydrodynamic quirk known to produce splats, squirts, submarines, and mystery moves.

San Isidro de El General is a delightful small town, lacking the congestion, sprawling development, and overwhelming diesel fumes of San José. This quaint municipality is the epitome of what urban geographers call a central place town. Its raison d'être is to serve the surrounding agricultural hinterland. San Isidro serves as the marketplace, source of goods and services, meeting place, and link to the outside world for the entire General valley. Only a minor village prior to the completion of the Pan-American Highway in the 1950s, it has boomed to a robust population of over 5000 today. Despite this vitality and recent growth, San Isidro maintains a village atmosphere, particularly on a Saturday night when villagers and peasants from many miles around swarm the central plaza, where musicians play and vendors sell fresh fruits, pastries, and tortillas from booths. San Isidro takes us back to a time and place where towns were service places for the surrounding countryside rather than vice versa.

Unlike the valley of the Pacuare, the majority of the General valley has been cleared for farming. It is an aesthetically pleasing landscape consisting primarily of extensive cattle ranches, although subsistence farming is common on the steep mountain slopes and Dole operates a huge pine-

Surfing at The BREW, Río General. Photo by Rafael Gallo.

apple plantation near Buenos Aires. These local, stem-ripened pineapples are immeasurably sweeter and tastier than those available in grocery stores in the States, so make it a point to stop at one of the roadside stands, restaurants, or fruit markets for a sample.

Some coffee, tobacco, sugar cane, corn, and rice are grown in the General valley. The landscape within the river corridor is dominated by open ranchland, with isolated remnants of forest. A liberal sprinkling of the aptly named royal palm tree gives the landscape a proper tropical ambience but it is the towering ceiba tree that dominates the riparian vegetation complex. These giants reach heights of 200 feet but it is their immense, heavily buttressed bases that first catch the eye. The ceiba is usually left uncut during deforestation because its wood is soft, low in durability, brittle when dry, and susceptible to fungus, although it is used for the construction of dugout canoes because the wood is so easily worked. Also, the local Indians hold the ceiba to be sacred and will not cut it. A planned airport in the valley was forced to relocate because the local populace refused to allow the trees at the proposed site to be cut. In addition to gracing the tropical river banks, the ceiba's seed pods contain the lightweight fiber known as kapok, the flotation material in cheap lifejackets.

The scenery along the General is superb; waterfalls cascade directly into the stream channel from high above and the river intermittently enters steep, narrow gorges that remain forested. Iguanas stretching three feet in length sunbathe on rocks and low ledges and the high peaks of the Cordillera de Talamanca loom to the northeast. Peasant children bathing in the river delight in seeing the gringos in their odd river craft and call out lyrical greetings and well wishes for the trip downstream. A trip down the General provides many exciting rapids and play spots but perhaps the most memorable aspects of a trip down this spectacular river are its stunning scenery and cultural delights. Long after the thrills of soaring enders and lengthy surfing excursions on the face of Chachalaca have subsided, glowing memories of royal palms, iguanas, ceiba trees, sparkling tropical skies, and radiant faces of peasant children remain.

# Río Chirripó Pacifico

**Section: Canaan to Rivas**
**Degree of Difficulty:** Class V, VI
**Gradient:** 211 feet per mile
**Length:** 5.6 miles
**Put-in Elevation:** 3870 feet
**Take-out Elevation:** 2690 feet
**Drainage Area:** 123 square miles
**Average Discharge:** 823 cfs
**Season:** Moderate water only—before and after the high-water peak of June through October

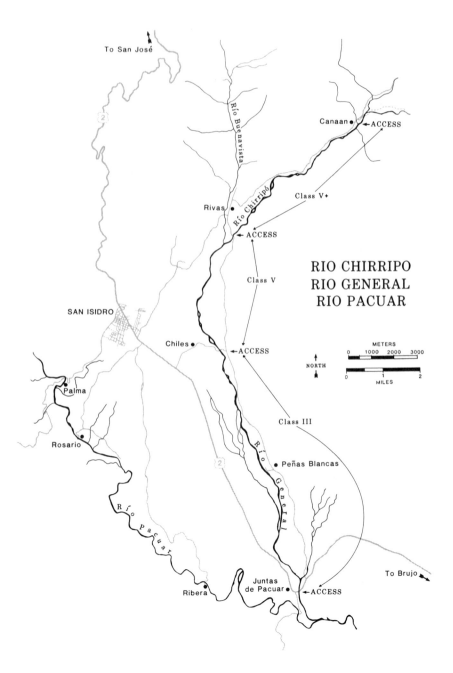

To San José

Río Buenavista

2

Canaan ● ←ACCESS

Class V+

Rivas ●

Río Chirripó

←ACCESS

Class V

**RIO CHIRRIPO
RIO GENERAL
RIO PACUAR**

SAN ISIDRO

Chiles ● ←ACCESS

METERS
0   1000   2000   3000

NORTH

0          1          2
MILES

Class III

Palma ●

Río General

2

● Peñas Blancas

Rosario ●

Río Pacuar

To Brujo →

Juntas
de Pacuar ● ←ACCESS

Ribera ●

Río General System   49

One need only examine the gradient of this section of river to get an idea of how difficult it is; the river drops at rates of up to 250 feet per mile in this short, intense section of the Chirripó (cheer uh PO). At the take-out for this section, the Chirripó merges with the Río Buenavista, thus forming the Río General. Despite what some whitewater rafters call it, the proper name for the river from this point downstream (until it joins the Coto Brus) is the Río General. This uppermost section of the river is extremely steep and difficult. It is recommended only for the most competent experts, with all possible precautions taken.

### Río Chirripó/Río General

**Section: Rivas to Chiles**
**Degree of Difficulty:** Class V
**Gradient:** 126 feet per mile
**Length:** 3.9 miles
**Put-in Elevation:** 2690 feet
**Take-out Elevation:** 2200 feet
**Drainage Area:** 200 square miles
**Average Discharge:** 823 cfs
**Season:** June through mid-December

This section of the Chirripó, while maintaining only one-half the gradient of the previous section, still contains some very difficult whitewater. The river is dropping over a boulder-laden course that provides continuous broaching opportunities. No portages are necessary, but neither are there many eddies to catch. The channel is quite narrow and large trees hanging over the river block the sun, adding to the difficulties and the sense of impending disaster.

Due to the continuous drops found in this section, it would not be prudent to paddle it at even moderately high water levels. Look for just enough water to provide clean passage through the rock jumbles.

# Río General

**Section: Chiles to Juntas de Pacuar**
**Degree of Difficulty:** Class III+
**Gradient:** 72 feet per mile
**Length:** 7.7 miles
**Put-in Elevation:** 2200 feet
**Take-out Elevation:** 1640 feet
**Drainage Area:** 250 square miles
**Average Discharge:** 1900 cfs
**Season:** June through December

In the eight-mile stretch between Chiles and the Pan-American Highway, the General drops through nearly continuous rapids and passes through scenery that boggles the mind of one who has recently arrived from the North. None of the drops are difficult but none of the pools are long. This section provides an ideal way to loosen up from the long drive over the mountains from San José, and often from a long period without paddling at all for those who have travelled from other countries to paddle here; the General is the first river on a week or ten-day excursion for many commercial trips. Initiates to tropical paddling are rewarded with warm water and outlandish scenery.

Halfway down this section, the river splits into two channels. The right side seems to disappear; take this channel. Here in the House of Horrors, the trees and reeds converge on the channel to completely conceal the river, where it passes through a vigorous Class III rapid. This is a wonderful place for anyone who is not claustrophobic.

Beyond the House of Horrors, the river becomes noticeably wider and the pools become somewhat longer. More houses are seen along the banks as you approach the town of Peñas Blancas. Despite these changes, the river still presents frequent rapids and the scenery is always pleasant.

The last significant rapid of the Chiles section is only one hundred yards above the take-out. Here the river drops over a broad ledge to

# RIO GENERAL

# JUNTAS - BRUJO

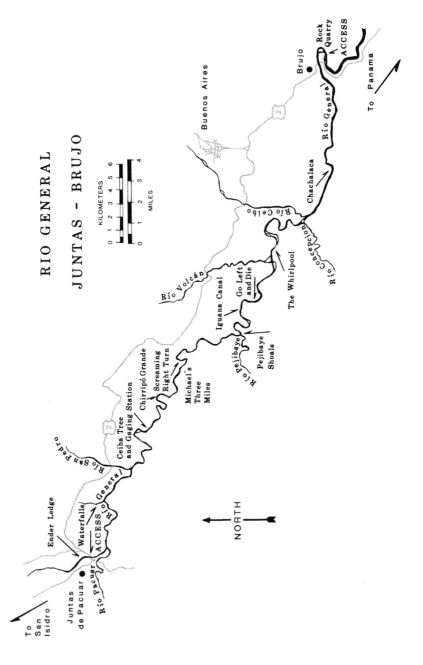

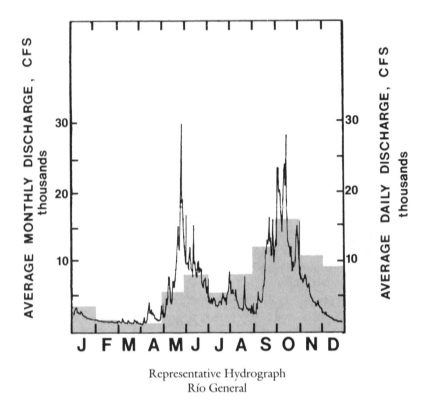

Representative Hydrograph
Río General

form a regular, but gentle, wave-hole that yields great side-surfing at low water and rocketing enders at high water levels.

Two primary tributaries feed the Upper General. When afternoon rains swell the flow of the upper tributary, it turns nearly black. The lower tributary turns a bright red-yellow color during the typical afternoon peak flow.

### Río General

**Section: Juntas de Pacuar to Brujo**
**Degree of Difficulty:** Class III, IV
**Gradient:** 28 feet per mile

**Length:** 43 miles
**Put-in Elevation:** 1640 feet
**Take-out Elevation:** 460 feet
**Drainage Area:** 927 square miles
**Average Discharge:** 7100 cfs (at take-out)
**Season:** May through December

The most constant characteristic of the General River is change. Beginning as a small mountain stream, the river immediately picks up its largest tributary, the Pacuar (not to be confused with the Atlantic drainage Pacuare). Substantial streams such as the Union, Pejibaye, Volcán, and Ceibo add their waters to the General at short intervals until it has become a brawny brown giant in the lower reaches. The river that is so small and intimate at the put-in is not recognizable as the same entity even 15 miles downstream. It is this constant change that gives the General its special character.

Beginning with a solid Class III rapid at the Pacuar junction, the main General is never boring. Even when the gradient eases up and the pools become fairly long, there is beautiful scenery in all directions. While lacking the spectacular aviary wonders of the Sarapiquí or Peñas Blancas, the General is the iguana capital of Costa Rica. These green reptiles grow to incredible sizes here and sun themselves on every available riverside ledge. The locals consider them to be a great delicacy, and call them *gallina de palo*—"tree chickens." The sight of a three-foot lizard running across the water in front of your boat is indeed a memorable one.

Four miles below the put-in, a tributary of moderate size plunges to the river from the left wall in a spectacular series of waterfalls. A short hike up this stream reveals even more waterfalls, deep pools, and dense, lush forest. There are many small, potentially runnable, tributaries which cascade into the General as well. The Union River joins the General at mile 6.3 below the Pan-American Highway.

The next big rapid is Elephant Rock, and is easily recognized by the large boulder for which the rapid is named. The preferred route here is to start left of the ledge at the top, then work to the right of the Elephant itself for the big drop. A long series of surfable waves follows the main drop; a convenient rest stop and eddy are on the right. A dozen or more Class II–III rapids follow in rapid succession.

At mile ten is a river gaging station and *the* ceiba tree. This tropical giant stands alone in a pasture, so it is hard to determine its true size until you stand next to it. Its massively buttressed base is at least 15 feet in diameter and the monster stands nearly 200 feet tall. Bromeliads hang from the upper limbs and ferns grow in the saddles between branches. This is one of the most impressive individual trees that you will ever see. The watershed of the General above this point has an area of 410 square miles and has an average discharge of 3100 cfs, but the average for October is 6900 cfs and the February average is but 610 cfs.

The next rapid of significance is deceptively dangerous. The river makes a broad bend to the left through a congested boulder field. The constant maneuvering at the top tends to divert the paddler's attention from a ledge at the bottom of the main chute. Even after recognizing the subtle horizon line, several paddlers have blundered ahead, unaware of the strength and severity of the hydraulic that lurks there until it was too late to avoid it. This hole should be avoided at all costs; start working toward the left bank long before reaching the bottom of the rapid.

Around the next bend is Chirripó Grande, one of the biggies. It is a long, complex rapid with several possible routes and plenty of opportunities to find trouble. This rapid is especially troublesome for rafts because a long hard ferry is needed to miss wrapping on one of the two huge boulders or flipping in one of the huge holes above and adjacent to the boulders. As water levels rise, this move becomes harder while the need to make it becomes more urgent. The preferable route here is to start center-left and work to the right, passing to the right of the first gargantuan boulder and to the left of the second. A second option at high water is to work *far* right all the way down through the scratchy stuff. This route avoids the big holes and boulders altogether.

A much-needed pool lies at the base of this Class IV+ drop and a beautiful beach is around the next bend on the left side of the river. Numerous Indian petroglyphs can be found on the dark boulders on a terrace above this beach. The site has not yet been studied by archaeologists and those who have studied photographs of the petroglyphs were unable to interpret them beyond noting that they are religious symbols.

Michael's Three Miles comes next. Okay, the name is somewhat of an exaggeration, but it does have a full mile of continuous Class III white-water. This section serves notice that Screaming Right Turn is just ahead. It isn't the turn that makes this rapid a screamer, but rather the huge pourover rock in the middle of the turn. The rock is right where the current tries to take a boat and there is enough water flowing over the obstacle that it does not create much of a pillow. Most hard boaters will want to cut hard right around the pourover, but the white-knuckle run is to the left, through the narrow notch between the rock wall and the pourover. Rafts will find it far easier to negotiate this narrow passage than to make a nearly impossible pull to the inside of the bend. At low water, the right side of the pourover produces dramatic enders from below but the hole behind the rock gets ugly even at moderate water levels.

The river opens up for several miles beyond this point and the rapids ease up. At the junction with the Pejibaye River, however, there is a very steep shoals rapid which offers dozens of possible routes. Find a clear one and go for it. The scenery here is remarkable looking back upstream. The rapid is perfectly framed by a steep verdant hillside with majestic royal palms sprinkled across it.

From the Pejibaye shoals to The Whirlpool is approximately six miles and in this distance are numerous rapids. The ones with names are, in order of occurrence, The Ramp, Forever Eddy, The BREW (the Best Rear Ender Wave), Iguana Canal, Go Left and Die, and The Crystal. The BREW offers superb surfing and enders, while the next two offer just what their names suggest. Iguana Canal is a section where the river flows between perched slivers of rock where the giant lizards sun themselves. Go Left and Die is a rather descriptive name that correctly implies what would likely happen to someone who missed the right-side route through this section of massive bedrock exposures. The left side has huge drops which terminate in ferocious hydraulics.

And now, folks, that special moment you've all been waiting for— The Whirlpool! If you haven't heard of The Whirlpool, you haven't talked to anyone who has paddled the General or read any of the numerous magazine articles about this magnificent hydraulic quirk. (Try the April 1984 issue of *Canoe* or the September 1986 issue of *River*

Pejibaye Shoals, Río General. Photo by Rafael Gallo.

*Runner.*) At this point the General pours over the right end of a massive ledge of resistant volcanic conglomerate. Behind the ledge is a huge eddy; the interaction of the surging water dropping over the ledge along a powerful eddy line creates a large vortex that spins downstream and obligingly pulls entire boats underwater for several seconds before dissipating. A new maelstrom forms every few seconds, so all that is required for catching it is a little timing or a little luck. Groups often spend two or three hours here spinning down the eddy line, giggling the afternoon away. Exhaustion ends most surfing sorties here rather than boredom.

Chachalaca, the other legendary surfing rapid, lies four miles downstream from The Whirlpool. There are two rapids in this stretch that would garner a lot of attention anywhere else on the river, but few people bother to explore their possibilities when the ultimate play wave is around the bend. After long anticipation, Chachalaca appears suddenly at a wide spot in the valley, where the river bends sharply to the left against a rock wall. To make matters more tense, this rapid is very hard to scout and the size and placement of the waves and holes cannot be determined until you are well into the rapid.

At low water levels, the main attraction at Chachalaca is a very tall, steep wave/hole that stretches across the river. It is ideally suited to side-surfing but it is so tall, steep, and continuous that many paddlers have a hard time breaking out of it once they have had their share of fun. A popped spray skirt will often do the trick if you are unable to stroke out of the left end. Be very careful not to turn over upstream in this hole; the ledge that produces it is quite shallow and poorly padded.

Greater runoff levels push the big hole farther and farther down-stream, while creating a beautifully sculpted standing wave that reaches enormous proportions when the river is running high and muddy. The

Mary Hipsher surfing Chachalaca, Río General. Photo by Rafael Gallo.

## Rating Table: General at El Brujo

| Gage height (meters) | Discharge (cfs) |
|---|---|
| 1.2 | 1600 |
| 1.4 | 2400 |
| 1.6 | 4000 |
| 1.8 | 4800 |
| 2.0 | 5900 |
| 2.2 | 7600 |
| 2.4 | 9500 |
| 2.6 | 11,700 |
| 2.8 | 14,000 |

Source: Compiled from Instituto Costarricense de Electricidad reports.

face grows to a length (not height) of over 20 feet, leaving more than enough room for a kayak to surf up and down its face as well as move laterally. In addition, the wave is steep enough to easily hold a boat against the force of onrushing water, allowing delicate changes in body position to determine the movement of the boat. To exit is as simple as sliding back over the lip, surfing out the side, or diving to the trough for a spectacular ender-exit. Don't forget that crashing hole downstream, however—you might want to save a little energy for getting out of it should it snare you. Some of the most experienced paddlers in the world consider this the ultimate play spot. Plan on spending a minimum of two hours here.

The last ten miles of the General tend to be somewhat anticlimactic, not because the river is without rapids or because the scenery is any less impressive, but simply because of fatigue and the natural tendency to be somewhat jaded by the magnitude of what has passed. The gradient from the mouth of the Ceibo to the take-out at Brujo does decline to 15 feet per mile, but some fairly challenging rapids remain. The pools between those rapids grow longer with each mile, however. When the river enters a steep, wooded canyon, only three miles remain. There is a narrow trail leading up to the road from the downstream left-hand side of the Pan-American Highway bridge at Brujo. Naturally, there is a bar at the top. The trail is too steep for rafts, so it is best for larger craft to continue another half-mile to a gravel quarry on the right.

Rafael Gallo surfing at The BREW, Río General. Photo by Victor Gallo.

Adequate flows for paddling the General are reliable from mid-May to December, and in many years the season lasts much longer than that. A minimum gage height of approximately 1.5 meters at El Brujo is needed, while many of the larger rapids become exceedingly difficult at levels above 2.4 meters. Excessive flows of short duration are not unusual during October and even November.

## Río Pacuar

**Section: Palma to Juntas de Pacuar**
**Degree of Difficulty:** Class II, III
**Gradient:** 32 feet per mile
**Length:** 15.3 miles

**Put-in Elevation:** 2100 feet
**Take-out Elevation:** 1600 feet
**Drainage Area:** 124 square miles at the take-out
**Average Discharge:** 1390 cfs
**Season:** June through December

Not to be confused with the Pacuare of the Atlantic drainage, the Pacuar is one of the major tributaries of the General. It runs parallel to the upper General, joining at Juntas de Pacuar (Pacuar Junction). Despite this proximity, the Pacuar is quite different from the General in its scenery, wildlife, and channel characteristics. This is one of the very few streams in Costa Rica that has bedrock ledges along its course, giving it a much different character. There is a lot of wildlife along this stream, including otters, hawks, kingfishers, and herons; the scenery and wildlife are reminiscent of the Sarapiquí.

From the put-in to the bridge at Rosario, the Pacuar has a modest gradient and rapids of Class I and II difficulty. In fact, it would be easier to use the put-in at Rosario, because the road is better and one misses only 2.3 miles of relatively uninteresting water. Below Rosario, the gradient increases to 37 feet per mile, with a pool-drop channel arrangement producing a number of interesting rapids. This section is ideal for beginners and intermediate paddlers, with many opportunities for surfing and even a couple of ender holes. In addition, it provides a good warm-up for the more rigorous demands of the main General.

The only drawback to running the Pacuar is that a coffee processing plant near Palma pours a heavy load of coffee effluent into the river on occasion. The discharge is not toxic by any means, but it smells bad. It would be wise to check the condition of the river at the take-out prior to putting in upstream.

As a general rule, the Pacuar is runnable between June and December, although flows are not entirely reliable in June and late December. The Pacuar is runnable when the gage at the take-out reads between 1.5 and 2.3 meters.

# Río Pacuare

The Pacuare (pa KWA ray) is the quintessential tropical river. Along its course lie several densely vegetated gorges, which shelter jaguars, ocelots, monkeys, sloths, and an incredible variety of birds. Also found within these gorges is some of the best whitewater in all of Central America, ranging up to Class V in difficulty. The Pacuare is the only river in Costa Rica that contains these amenities, including virgin rain forest, while also being quite accessible. Other rivers such as the Telire and the Chirripó Atlantico can match the attractions of the Pacuare but require either a multi-day carry-in or the services of a helicopter.

There are several access points along the Pacuare other than the ones described below, but we believe these to be the best. The road to Tres Equis is convenient but it is privately owned and it will cost you a substantial fee to use it. The oxcart put-in gives an extra two miles of good rapids at a much lower cost: either a 1.7-mile carry or a small fee for the oxcart.

Unfortunately, this tropical utopia is threatened in the long term by the deforestation that is rampant throughout the tropical rain forests of Latin America and in the very near term by governmental plans to construct a massive hydroelectric dam at Dos Montanas. The narrow gorge at Dos Montanas is, no doubt, the dam builder's dream. Through this narrow cleft flows a river with a large, dependable flow (average of 2200 cfs) and the gorge itself provides an ideal dam site. Completion of this project would, no doubt, supply a number of jobs during construction and a valuable commodity afterwards but invaluable resources would be lost. If the 267-meter dam is completed, it will inundate the lower gorge all the way upstream to the Tres Equis put-in, along with its spectacular waterfalls, Indian villages, and precious wildlife habitat. In addition, it is questionable whether the electricity produced is needed. The recently completed diversion projects on the Arenal River have nearly doubled the country's output of electricity; the ability of the domestic market to absorb a substantial increase in output during a period of slow economic growth is dubious. Efforts to protect the lower gorge of the Pacuare by inclusion as part of Costa Rica's exemplary national park system are moving ahead sluggishly. We desperately hope that either preservationist legislation or economic conditions will force abandonment of this project. Those concerned with preservation of this unique river and the jungle wilderness around it should write to the president of Costa Rica:

President Calderon
P.O. Box 283-2100
Zapote, Costa Rica


## Río Pacuare

**Section: Bajo Pacuare to San Martin**
**Degree of Difficulty:** Class V, VI
**Gradient:** 76 feet/mile (3 @ 94 feet/mile) (0.6 @ 109)
**Length:** 15 miles
**Put-in Elevation:** 1900 feet
**Take-out Elevation:** 950 feet
**Drainage Area:** 142 square miles
**Average Discharge:** 1300 cfs
**Season:** All year

This spectacular section of the Pacuare is one of the world's great whitewater treasures but its length, difficulty, and isolation preclude all but the most determined and skilled paddlers from attempting it. Fifteen miles of paddling on water of such difficulty, with three likely portages, make for a very nearly impossible single-day descent. Carrying camping gear in boats makes this Class V run all the more difficult. In addition, the take-out at San Martin is 1.7 miles from the river, with a steep rutted path being the only means of egress. An excellent option is, of course, to continue downstream through the scenic lower canyons. The difficulty lies in carrying sufficient gear for a three-day trip in a boat while negotiating the extremely difficult rapids of the upper section. We recommend arranging for raft support from San Martin to Siquirres.

Río Pacuare below Tres Equis. Photo by Rafael Gallo.

Almost all of the difficult rapids in this section occur within two steep-walled canyons, each of which is separated by more open sections where the canyon walls are not as steep or confining. If difficulties should arise, it would be best to continue downstream or return upstream to one of the open areas to hike out on the left bank (there are only a few isolated farms for 100 miles from river right). One could easily depart on foot from Bajo Pacuare number two, six miles downstream from the put-in, or with greater difficulty at any one of several small clusters of houses.

The upper and lower Pacuare were first run by the Polish Canoandes expedition in 1980. Led by Piotr Chmielinski, the group paddled the difficult upper gorges during the high-water month of September, making this among the most difficult rivers that the expedition attempted.

Michael Shulte, a river ranger on the Middle Fork of the Salmon, led two other kayakers on the next descent of the upper Pacuare in 1983. They portaged three rapids that were described as Class V–VI and named several of the rapids in the gorge. The third trip down this section was inadvertent. A group of rafters from the United States put in at Bajo Pacuare, thinking that this was the correct launch site for the main Pacuare run. Fortunately, the group consisted of experienced rafters who had the sense to scout whenever the river became difficult and to portage several of the more difficult drops.

Whitewater photographer Tom Stults, Fernando Castaneda, and Rafael Gallo were the next group to attempt this section of the Pacuare, relying on Michael Shulte's detailed river notes. The group managed to run the first Class V–VI drop and obtained photographs of this remarkable river.

For the first mile and one-half below Bajo Pacuare, the river flows through open fields where small farms reach to the river's edge. Small houses line the river and many fishermen are seen along the banks. Suddenly, the river bends hard to the left and becomes very congested. Difficult rapids quickly replace the houses as the most common streamside features and few signs of human occupancy are found. The rapids are very steep boulder gardens replete with powerful holes. The first one can be boat scouted but each consecutive rapid seems to increase in congestion, power, and difficulty. Several of them have badly undercut sidewalls and nearly every one of them requires a lot of maneuvering between house-sized boulders and large holes. One such rapid has similar features to the previous ones, only carried to an extreme. Most parties carry it, but it has been run by starting far left, then working to the far right where two monster holes must be punched.

The river opens up somewhat after approximately five miles, then the rapids are fairly easy until the small village of Bajo Pacuare appears on the left. A hanging bridge upstream from Bajo Pacuare signals the end of the first difficult section.

Two miles of easy paddling brings you to a marked canyon, where the largest drops on the upper Pacuare are found. Most parties make their second portage in this stretch at Jumping Bobo Falls, which has a Class V+ rapid above it. The rapid is named for the bobo fish, which

Running the hole at Upper Huacas, Río Pacuare. Moderately high water level. Photos by Rafael Gallo.

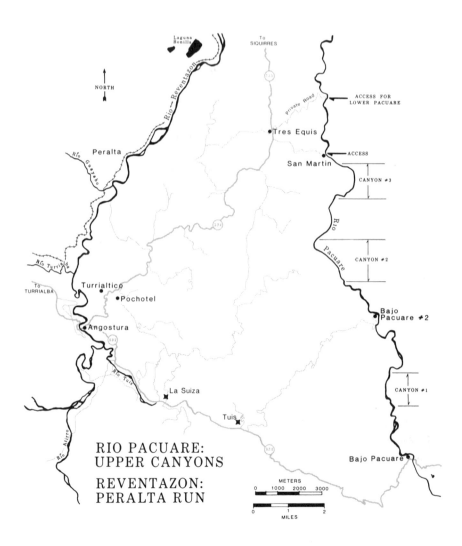

RIO PACUARE:
UPPER CANYONS

REVENTAZON:
PERALTA RUN

migrates upstream to reproduce. The ten-foot falls are a major obstacle to their migration, and they can often be seen making spectacular leaps to clear the cataract. The rapid above would be only marginally runnable without the tree jammed in it, the huge undercut rock at its left, or the waterfall at its end. When Rafael attempted the rapid on his first run, he was pulled beneath the undercut by the tremendous force of the river and disappeared for an extended period. Fernando was manning a safety line, which Rafael managed to grab just before washing over the waterfall. His boat remained lodged under the boulder for several more minutes before washing out. Earl Alderson accomplished the first and possibly the last "successful" run of the falls in 1984. He managed to find a clean line over the edge, using a powerful stroke to clear the drop, only to be endered and severely thrashed in the reversal at the bottom. A few individuals have managed successful runs through the entrance rapid but few others have attempted the falls.

### Río Pacuare

**Section: San Martin to Siquirres**
**Degree of Difficulty:** Class III (IV)
**Gradient:** 46 feet per mile
**Length:** 16.3 miles
**Put-in Elevation:** 950 feet
**Take-out Elevation:** 195 feet
**Drainage Area:** 254 square miles at take-out
**Average Discharge:** 2200 cfs
**Season:** All year

One of the most memorable aspects of the Pacuare trip is the put-in. Local *campesinos* shuttle rafts, kayaks, equipment, and food 1.7 miles down a dirt path on an oxen-drawn cart. The middle Meadow River take-out could use such a rig. Along the way to the river, the trail passes a small mill for processing sugar cane. The juice extracted from the cane is used to make sugar or the powerful white liquor known as *guaro*. The friendly natives may offer a sample. You'll be far better off if they do not.

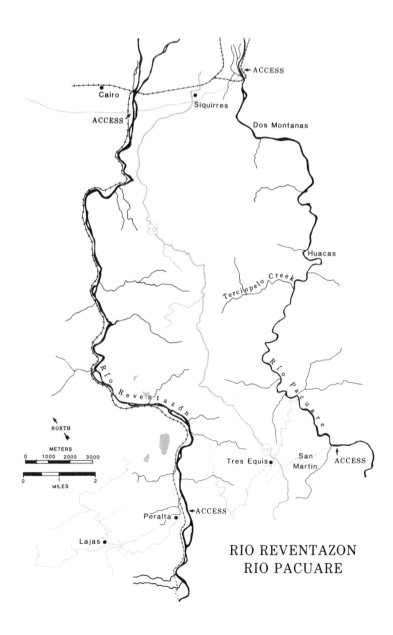

ACCESS

Cairo

Siquirres

ACCESS

Dos Montanas

Huacas

Terciopelo Creek

Río Pacuare

Río Reventazón

NORTH

METERS
0    1000   2000   3000

0                        2
MILES

Tres Equis

San
Martin

ACCESS

ACCESS

Peralta

Lajas

RIO REVENTAZON
RIO PACUARE

From the put-in to the beginning of the inner gorge, the river drops through numerous Class II–III boulder gardens and simple drops as it becomes sequestered in the ever more verdant rain forest. The big cats are rarely seen, but somehow you just know that they are watching you warily from the dark shadows of the enclosing jungle. Many parties camp at a semi-abandoned riverside farm on a low terrace five miles below the put-in. Hundreds of parakeets living in a huge tree in the midst of the clearing provide entertainment, but grazing cattle tend to be a nuisance. Several smaller camps offer equivalent amenities, including trails through the verdant jungle and easy access to nearby waterfalls.

Around the next bend, the river is pinched to one-half its former width by steep rock walls; it is here that the intriguing inner gorge begins. After another mile, Terciopelo ("velvet") Creek cascades in from river left. Take the time for a hike up its canyon, where numerous waterfalls and plunge pools await the adventurous. After Terciopelo Creek, the Pacuare continues through another one and one-half miles of jungle before reaching the zenith of this whitewater fantasyland: the Huacas rapids. Upper Huacas is a Class III+ drop through a congested boulder garden. It presents no real difficulties for kayaks but rafts must maneuver carefully at the top to avoid boulder pins. At certain water levels, a particularly grabby hole develops at the base of the rapid. It is known as Traitor Hole, and even expert kayakers have been forced to swim out of it.

Just beyond the end of the rapid, a most incredible sight appears: a tributary stream plunges over a 150-foot free-fall directly into the Pacuare. Above the main drop, the small stream recedes from sight in a series of small waterfalls encased in slickrock walls. The sight of Huacas Falls alone is worth a trip to Costa Rica.

Another 200 yards downstream, the lower Pacuare produces its toughest rapid: Lower Huacas. Even at low water levels, this 150-yard stretch of ledges and boulders is a solid Class IV rapid. At higher water, the holes become voracious, the pools microscopic, and the right-side portage tempting.

Beyond Lower Huacas are several Class III rapids but none of difficulty comparable to Lower Huacas. The canyon opens up gradually

One of the many waterfalls on the Pacuare. Photo by Rafael Gallo.

after another two miles and rapids become easier and more widely spaced, with one exception. Cimarron Rapid is a steep boulder garden through which the river disperses into multiple channels. Kayaks can negotiate the rapid with relative ease, but rafts have a very difficult time of it, for frequent changes of course are required to avoid wrapping on one of the numerous boulders.

At a deep pool in the river some five miles past Lower Huacas, a sandy beach appears on the right. A short hike up the trail from the beach reveals a small Indian village of grass huts and small gardens. These indigenous people are true subsistence farmers. All of their food is grown in their fields, gathered in the forest, or caught from the river itself. The huts are made entirely from the wood and leaves of the Cola de Gallo palm, one of the few woods that resist the rapid decay brought on by the perennial warm, moist conditions of the Atlantic lowlands.

The river is littered with dark remnants of young basaltic lava flows in the stretch beyond the Indian village. Fantastic geometric forms speak of the forces of contraction during cooling and subsequent weathering that have altered these stone monoliths. As the river's gradient decreases and the valley becomes wider, more and more traces of man are seen: larger fields of crops and occasional huts are encountered. The river has one last set of wonders to awe the newcomer to this land, however: Dos Montanas, the rapid and the canyon. The rapid begins as a boulder garden, sweeping from right to left and ends in a set of large standing waves, several of which are suitable for extended surfing. One hundred yards downstream stands the river's last spectacle: the deep cleft known as Dos Montanas Gorge. As the name suggests, two mountains pinch the river into a narrow defile. The mighty Pacuare has done its work effectively, however. It has cut cleanly through the obstacle, leaving no rapids in the gorge. The Pacuare runs in eerie quietness through the rock-walled gorge as if to evade by secrecy the fate designed for it by the hydroelectric engineers. Preliminary work on the dam site has already commenced, with bulldozers desecrating the beauty of one of the world's most majestic canyons. We recommend that you carefully scout Dos Montanas Rapid and the entrance to the gorge because of the possibility of encountering a logjam from the construction work.

All that remains now is an anticlimactic Class II–III paddle of two and a half miles to the take-out under the Limón–San José highway bridge. Far from being boring, however, this section opens up new vistas of tropical agriculture and distant mountains. As the adrenaline level recedes and weariness settles in, one finally has the opportunity to reflect on the scenic wonders of the Pacuare River and the dam that will soon destroy them all.

The Pacuare was first paddled by the Polish Canoandes expedition in 1980. The participants included Piotr Chmielinski, Jerzy Majcherczyk, Zbigniew Bzdak, Jacek Boguki, Andrzej Pietowski, and Jarostaw Samsel.

The rating table indicates discharge values corresponding to various gage readings from the gage station at Dos Montanas. Unfortunately, there is no convenient gage for streamflow determination at the put-in. Minimum discharge levels for a raft trip down the gorge are in the 800–1000 cfs range but kayak and canoe trips at lower levels are quite enjoyable. As the accompanying hydrograph indicates, substantial flows are almost always available from June until December, and occasional flows of above 1000 cfs occur even during the dry season. Trips during January, February, and March do not provide the whitewater thrills of the wet season, but the exquisite scenery, abundant wildlife, and clear water more than compensate for the loss of action. Excessive water levels occasionally interfere with paddling, primarily during the month of October. A reasonable upper limit would be approximately 6000 cfs.

### Rating Table: Pacuare at Dos Montanas

| Gage Height (meters) | Discharge (cfs) |
| --- | --- |
| 1.9 | 425 |
| 2.0 | 600 |
| 2.1 | 980 |
| 2.2 | 1300 |
| 2.3 | 1700 |
| 2.4 | 2250 |
| 2.5 | 2800 |
| 2.6 | 3500 |
| 2.7 | 4200 |
| 2.8 | 4900 |
| 2.9 | 5700 |
| 3.0 | 7000 |

Source: Compiled from Instituto Costarricense de Electricidad reports.

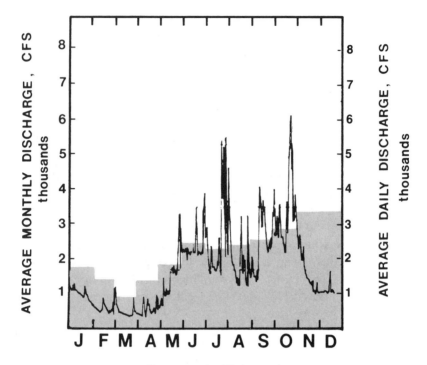

Representative Hydrograph
Río Pacuare at Dos Montanas

# Reventazón System

The Reventazón (ruh venta ZOHN) gathers its waters from the rugged core of the Cordillera de Talamanca. Some of the upper tributaries drain the wettest parts of the country. By the time they have gathered enough volume to float a boat but have lost enough gradient so as not to destroy one, the river still is at an elevation of almost 4000 feet. Whitewater can be found on the Reventazón all the way to Siquirres, at an elevation of 150 feet. The entire reach of runnable whitewater is 60 miles long, rivaling the length of the General. Within the Reventazón system are the Grande de Orosi, the Pejibaye, the Reventazón itself, and many small tributaries that have not yet been paddled. After its junction with the Navarro, the Orosi is known as the Reventazón, an appropriate name meaning "bursting waves." The river lives up to its name along much of its length.

The Reventazón watershed drains a part of the eastern slope of the Cordillera Central which gathers very high annual rainfall totals and occasionally receives very heavy afternoon and evening rainfall. As a result, even the mainstem of the Reventazón is subject to sudden dramatic increases in discharge. A raft trip on the Reventazón experienced a two-meter rise in water level while paddling the Tucurrique section in August of 1987. The higher flows made for a more enjoyable cruise down this section of the river but would have required abandoning the lower Peralta section. Contingency plans for such possibilities should be arranged during the rainy season.

## Río Grande de Orosi

During the high-water season of October 1984, Kevin Knussmann, Fernando Castaneda, Tom Wise, and Oswaldo Trejos attempted the uppermost section of the Orosi (or ROW see), putting in at road's end above Tapanti, at the mouth of the Río Dos Amigos. The river flows through a gorge of incredible beauty in this uppermost section, but the gradient is over 200 feet per mile in the first three miles, and the difficulty of this section is even greater than the gradient implies.

There are at least a dozen rapids and waterfalls that should be portaged in the Refugio Tapanti section, including a double drop of over 50 feet that requires a long rope and steady nerves to portage, for the canyon walls are steep and very slippery. The first descent group managed to run drops of 8 feet, 13 feet, and 16 feet, but the 8-foot ledge breaks onto poorly padded rocks and Kevin was briefly held in a vertical pin. In addition to these "small" drops, the group encountered a 30-foot waterfall whose plunge pool quickly led into a second drop of 20 feet. The group managed to portage the double drop with considerable difficulty and reported that even that would have been impossible with only a little more water. They finally ended the trip at Palomo after dark, having averaged only one mile per hour. This section of river is extremely hazardous; none of the four who have run it are willing to consider a second attempt at any water level. Neil Kahn, the only other person who has paddled this section, will only commit to running it again *mañana*.


### Río Grande de Orosi

**Section: Tapanti to Palomo**
**Degree of Difficulty:** Class V, VI
**Gradient:** 104 feet per mile, 0.4 @ 170 feet per mile
**Length:** 3.3 miles
**Put-in Elevation:** 3920 feet
**Take-out Elevation:** 3575 feet
**Drainage Area:** 143 square miles at take-out
**Average Discharge:** 1230 cfs
**Season:** July through December, intermittently

On (map) paper this looks like an ideal section to paddle; it has easy access, a steep but manageable gradient of 105 feet per mile, and the sections visible from the road are obviously runnable. Beyond the first bend, however, the river enters a small gorge. The gradient quickly

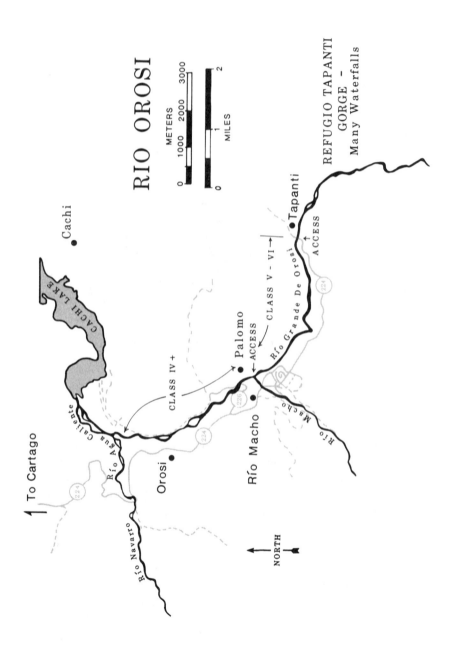

RIO OROSI

METERS

0    1000    2000    3000

MILES

0        1        2

To Cartago

Cachi

CACHI LAKE

Agua Caliente

Río Navarro

Orosi

Río Macho

Río Macho

Palomo

CLASS IV +

ACCESS

CLASS V – VI

Río Grande De Orosi

224

226

224

Tapanti

ACCESS

REFUGIO TAPANTI
GORGE –
Many Waterfalls

NORTH

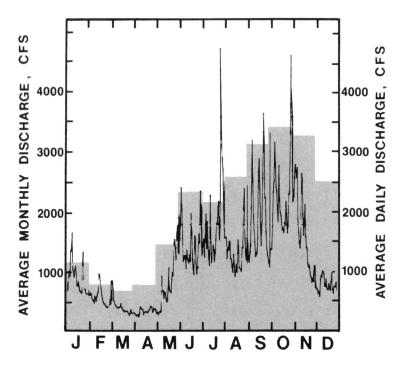

Representative Hydrograph
Río Grande de Orosi

increases to 120, then 173 feet per mile as the drops become large bedrock ledges. The first significant rapid on this section begins where the river bends to the right into a maze of boulders. This is a mandatory portage, preferably from the right side. This rapid is only 25 yards long, but it is followed by another Class VI rock jumble, so the entire portage is about 75 yards long.

The river now settles down to mere Class V, with many radical but runnable drops until the current is divided by an island. The right side is marginally runnable (Class V+). Finally, the difficulty of the rapids decreases considerably, with only one difficult rapid, another Class VI, after the island. Two hundred yards past that final portage is a hot spring area on the left that is useful for soothing sore backs and shoulders that have been abused by the numerous portages. There are no more difficult rapids until the junction with Río Macho.


### Río Grande de Orosi

**Section:** Palomo to Cachi Lake
**Degree of Difficulty:** Class IV, V
**Gradient:** 90 feet per mile
**Length:** 3 miles
**Put-in Elevation:** 3575 feet
**Take-out Elevation:** 3315 feet
**Drainage Area:** 143 square miles at put-in
**Average Discharge:** 1230 cfs
**Season:** August through November

This section of river was first rafted in July 1984 by a crew led by Jimmy Nixon and Rafael Gallo. They found the run from Palomo to Cachi Lake to contain continuous Class IV whitewater at low to moderate water levels but peak flows of September and October frequently turn the first two miles into a nearly continuous Class V torrent.

The Orosi gains two major tributaries in this stretch, gaining a considerable volume of water. The cascading Río Macho joins the Orosi at the Palomo put-in, then the flatter but larger Río Agua Caliente joins the mainstream one mile above Cachi Lake. Neither tributary is large enough to paddle but the added volume of water does make a noticeable difference in the river. Unfortunately, a more noticeable difference that the Agua Caliente makes is in water quality, as it carries a heavy load of pollution from the Cartago area. It is best to take out as soon as possible after passing the mouth of the Agua Caliente.

The easiest put-in for this section is at the bridge between the towns of Río Macho and Palomo but there are two excellent rapids just upstream, most notably Neil's Back Yard. It is easy to put in just above these rapids from the left side of the river. Just above the bridge is an interesting rapid named La Palma, which lies directly below Motel Rio. Motel Rio is a favorite place for kayakers to stay when paddling the

### Rating Table: Río Grande de Orosi at Palomo

| Gage Height (meters) | Discharge (cfs) |
| --- | --- |
| 1.0 | 200 |
| 1.1 | 280 |
| 1.2 | 430 |
| 1.3 | 600 |
| 1.4 | 820 |
| 1.5 | 1100 |
| 1.6 | 1450 |
| 1.7 | 1800 |

Source: Compiled from Instituto Costarricense de Electricidad reports.

Orosi. The next rapid is very long, very busy, and a lot of fun: Verano Sin Fin ("Endless Summer"). Others know this rapid as Quiebra Cocos ("the Head Buster").

The entrance of Río Navarro from the left signals the end of the steep, difficult section of the Orosi, and the headwaters of the reservoir are only a mile downstream. Easy take-outs are found all along the right bank. Most boaters run this section at least twice in a day because it is relatively short and the shuttle is easy—a dirt road follows the river down the right bank throughout the run. Watch for guava trees along the road on the way back to the put-in, for their fruit makes a great snack between runs. The trunk of the guava tree has brown peeling bark; it has small leaves, and fruit about the size of a lime. When the fruit is ripe, it changes from green to slightly yellow.

# Río Reventazón

**Section:** Cachi Dam to El Congo Powerhouse (Canon Section)
**Degree of Difficulty:** Class IV, V, VI
**Gradient:** 108 feet per mile
**Length:** 6.4 miles
**Put-in Elevation:** 3085 feet

**Take-out Elevation:** 2395 feet
**Drainage Area:** 165 square miles
**Average Discharge:** 600 cfs (when running)
**Season:** Wet season only—dam overflow releases

Stretching a brief 6.4 miles from the base of Cachi Dam to the point where the penstocks return the dam's impounded waters to their natural channel, the Canon de Reventazón is nonetheless isolated, scenic, and difficult to paddle. The gorge is dry most of the year, since the river's flow is diverted to the powerhouse at El Congo, where 20 percent of the nation's electricity is produced. When flows of the Orosi exceed storage capacity in the lake and the penstocks' capacity, water is released into the dry gorge. Discharge values can be obtained at the dam; a minimum of 10 cms (350 cfs) is required and the section has been paddled with a discharge as high as 17 cubic meters per second.

The trip begins at the dam spillway, with an impressive view of the canyon below. In the first mile, the river's gradient is moderate and it is possible to enjoy the scenery, as the river winds through narrow canyons which open up into lush fields of coffee and sugar cane above. The channel changes character dramatically in the second and third miles, with a much steeper gradient and considerable debris from dam construction producing tight, congested rapids. With most of the streamflow diverted through the penstocks to the lower powerhouse, the Reventazón does not flood frequently enough or high enough to clear out this debris. Great care should be exercised here to avoid steel rebar, railroad ties, and angular rock fragments produced during the construction of the dam.

At the entrance to the first main rapid, it is necessary to paddle through a two-foot-wide slot between a boulder and a piece of rebar that points upstream. Beyond an eddy, the rapid really gets serious, with the river dropping over a set of three consecutive eight-foot drops. The line to take here is to begin on the left, move to the center eddy, then work to the right all the way down; the final drop is taken against the right wall. One cannot help but worry here about the possibility of more rebar lurking below the frothing water of one of these drops. The rest of

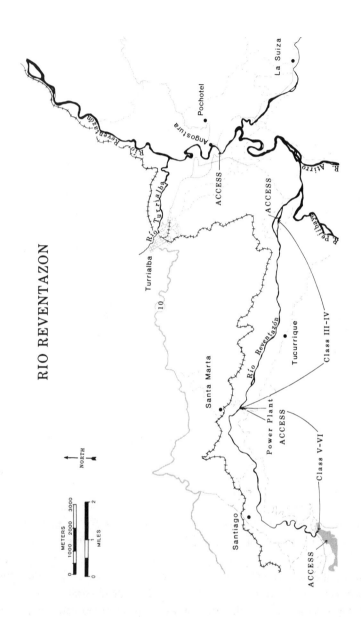

# RIO REVENTAZON

NORTH

METERS
0  1000  2000  3000

MILES
0        1        2

La Suiza

Pochotel

Angostiura

R. Atirro

Rio Reventazom

Rio Turrialba

Turrialba

10

ACCESS

ACCESS

R. Pejibaye

Santa Marta

Rio Reventazón

Tucurrique

Class III-IV

Power Plant
ACCESS

Class V-VI

Santiago

ACCESS

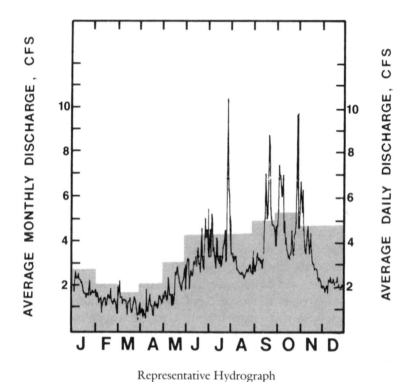

Representative Hydrograph
Río Reventazón

the run features a continuous gradient, with many difficult rapids. A great deal of maneuvering is necessary to avoid pourover rocks and powerful hydraulics. Most of the rapids can be boat-scouted but be prepared for a lot of cross-river traverses to avoid danger spots.

### Río Reventazón

**Section: Cachi Powerhouse to Angostura**
**Degree of Difficulty:** Class III, IV
**Gradient:** 57 feet per mile, 1.2 @ 110 feet per mile
**Length:** 12.6 miles

**Put-in Elevation:** 2427 feet
**Take-out Elevation:** 1706 feet
**Drainage Area:** 339 square miles at put-in
                       516 square miles at take-out
**Average Discharge:** 1800 cfs at put-in
                             3600 cfs at take-out
**Season:** All year

From the put-in at the powerhouse to the small bridge outside Tucurrique, a distance of a little over three miles, the Reventazón drops relentlessly at a rate of 85 feet per mile, with the first mile dropping more than 115 feet. With an average discharge of 1800 cfs in the channel, such a gradient would ordinarily produce Class V–VI water, but the Reventazón is a manageable Class IV run because the gradient is so steady; there are only very short pools in this upper section between the drops. In fact, the daytime discharge of the penstocks is closer to 3000 cfs; the average discharge listed above includes the nighttime periods when little or no water is being released. This is big water, at least in comparison to the Orosi or the Pacuare.

The first two drops on the river are the most difficult, because both are in blind curves and must be paddled without any warm-up. The first begins immediately after the put-in, where the river swings right to left through tall, dense grasses that block the view downstream. There are two large pourover rocks in the middle of the channel that must be avoided. Around the next corner the river splits around an island, with the majority of the river flowing down the right side. The river bends from left to right, then drops over a very steep bouldery drop at the end of the island. To run this rapid successfully, one must paddle from center-left at the top to far right, then quickly snap the boat around to the left again to take the big bouldery drop. This is the only single drop on the river that deserves a solid Class IV rating. Beyond the big drop, the river plunges over a delightful series of rapids. None of them is difficult but it is hard to find such a continuous run of whitewater anywhere else.

Beyond Tucurrique, the river's gradient eases up considerably. The pools grow longer, the canyon opens up, and several large tributaries swell the river's flow. The last eight miles of the river are quite scenic, with intermittent views of the Turrialba volcano and expansive agricultural operations. The bridge at Angostura provides a convenient take-out.

An ideal ending to a day on the Reventazón is to take a short drive from the take-out to one of the two nearby mountainside restaurants, Pochotel or Turrialtico. Each offers fine food, cold drinks, and an outstanding view of the Reventazón Valley, the town of Turrialba, and the CATIE research center. In addition, they usually allow paddlers to camp on their front lawn. An exciting, demanding day on the river earns you a cold drink on the veranda with a commanding view of the Reventazón Valley, flocks of egrets flying in formation, and the dominating mass of Turrialba Volcano on the skyline.

In many ways, the main Reventazón is similar to the Ocoee River of Tennessee; it is dam-controlled, has moderately difficult whitewater, and its water quality leaves something to be desired. The generation schedule of the power plant at El Congo assures a steady flow of water during the day, when electrical demand is high. This dependability of flow, coupled with its proximity to the Central Valley, makes it the most heavily used whitewater river in the country, although it is unlikely that you will see another group of paddlers on the river. The water quality of the Reventazón is not up to the high standards of some of the other nearby rivers such as the Orosi or Pacuare due to the fact that the Reventado and its tributaries deliver a heavy load of pollutants from the Cartago urban area. Some of the pollutants settle out in Cachi Lake but the river sometimes has a noticeable odor at the put-in. Fortunately, the steep gradient of the river ensures rapid oxygenation of the waters and the flow is diluted by the merging waters of the Pejibaye, Atirro, and Túis rivers so that the Reventazón is noticeably cleaner below Tucurrique.

Beginning rafters and intermediate paddlers may wish to put in at Tucurrique in order to miss the difficult rapids in the first three to four miles. What remains is beautiful scenery, varied wildlife, and Class III whitewater.

# Río Reventazón

**Section: Angostura to Peralta**
**Degree of Difficulty:** Class V
**Gradient:** 68 feet per mile, 2 miles @ 85 feet per mile
**Length:** 9.1 miles
**Put-in Elevation:** 1706 feet
**Take-out Elevation:** 1394 feet
**Drainage Area:** 516 square miles
**Average Discharge:** 3800 cfs
**Season:** All year (too high during rainy season)

Legendary for its big water and big drops, this section contains some of the heaviest whitewater in Central America. It has been compared to the classic big-water run of the East, the Upper Gauley of West Virginia, and there are indeed many similarities. The Peralta section of the Reventazón would have to be considered a notch above the Gauley in difficulty due to its higher gradient and continuous action, however. This is not a section of river that lends itself to unguided first attempts; there are mandatory lines to be made in each of the big drops and few of them are apparent from a fast-moving boat.

The river flows through an intimate canyon through the first three miles of this section, with few access points along the way. A nice view of this upper section can be obtained from the front porch of Pochotel or Turrialtico. The first half-mile of the run provides an easy warm-up for the rigors ahead, as the river drops through several mild Class III rapids. The serious action ahead is heralded by The Play Wave, a.k.a., Angelica. The surfing is great, but be sure to save plenty of energy for the big rapids that begin just around the corner. The next mile is known as The Meatgrinder section, for this is where the ravioli hits the fan. It contains six major rapids, each separated by a pool large enough for a brief recovery but little else. The largest and most dangerous of the six is Jungle Run, and fortunately, it is easily recognized. At the end of a short, powerful drop is a right-hand eddy of huge proportions, which swirls up against a jagged rock wall. The river meanders around this wall, with a Class V drop on the left bank and the Class VI Jungle Run on the inside of the bend; a low island separates the two chutes. The Jungle Run has been paddled several times but it is not recommended. Scouting is a must here and portaging down the left bank is relatively easy. The left side "Chicken Route" used to be the preferred option, but it has become so clogged with debris that it is rarely runnable. The only option for paddling this rapid may be the Jungle Run. The river flows into a narrow canyon with huge boulders and massive holes. You will need a lot of skill and good fortune to make this run.

After the Jungle Run come Royal Flush and Colador. Both are powerful rapids but significantly less threatening than Jungle Run. Several more large drops follow, each of which is of Class IV+ to V in difficulty. After 2.6 miles (4.2 km), the Turrialba River enters from the left bank. Unfortunately, the Turrialba delivers a fairly high load of pollutants from the city of the same name that is just upstream. This ends the CATIE section, named for the research institution which controls the land along the left bank of the river throughout this section. The CATIE center has gained an international reputation for their research in tropical agronomy and forestry and the CATIE run is quickly gaining an international reputation in the paddling community for the incredible rapids and reliable flows which characterize this short section of the Reventazon. Those wishing to end their runs at this point must take out on river left and walk about half of a mile (.8 km) by way of Bajo Chino to a dirt road that leads to Turrialba and Angostura.

As the Turrialba enters, the canyon opens up but the gradient decreases only slightly and the rapids change somewhat in character. In this lower section, the drops tend to be longer, wider, and contain more ledges and holes. Few of the rapids have yet earned names, but there are at least 30 rapids with difficulty factors of Class IV and above.

The first major section of rapids consists of a long series of S-turns with very short pools between the drops. It is known as Piedras de Fuego, "Rocks of Fire". The last drop in Piedras de Fuego has a serious ledge hole on the right side that can be avoided by moving to the left while negotiating the rapid. It was named for a near-calamity. The fourth or fifth of a series of nearly identical drops, it contains a monster hole that stretches across most of the main chute. Even those who have run this section repeatedly watch warily for The Hole in every drop before the monster finally appears. On one of the inaugural runs, a kayaker had the misfortune of swimming the lower half of the rapid. As he dropped over the ledge and spotted the gaping abyss, he quickly planted his feet on the ledge, rose, and dove powerfully into the hole. His dramatic dive succeeded in plunging him into the deep outwash and his companions immediately dubbed the drop The Swan Dive. To avoid such drama, stay in your boat and stay left at any cost.

The second of the named rapids in this lower stretch is Lava Central (some call it "El Horrendo"), and it is well worthy of either name. The river focuses all of its considerable energy on the center of the channel, as the river drops 20 to 25 feet (6-7 m) over a distance of 75 yards (70 m). There is a large hole in the middle of the channel that can be skirted on the left, or one may choose the hero route through the middle of it at the right water level. Enormous waves converge and crash unpredictably while violent surging currents thrust boats in all directions. This is probably the single most distinctive rapid in all of Costa Rica.

The next named rapid, La Ceja, is similar to Lava Central in size and character but it is longer, wider, and somewhat less disorienting. After a fairly long straight approach, the river bends to the right. The main channel begins far right and angles slightly to the left.

The Peralta run ends with a bang, not a whimper: the last rapid is known as the Land of A Thousand Holes, and for good reason. The rapid has no discernable line to run; the only option is to plunge in and hope to react quickly enough to avoid being trapped in one of the many hydraulic obstacles. Three of the holes in this rapid are especially dangerous, so scout the rapid carefully or follow someone who has paddled the river recently.

The take-out for this section is on the left beneath the suspended foot bridge near the end of Land of A Thousand Holes. That's right—not shortly after the rapid, but in the rapid, so have your act together if the water is high. The train is no longer available for shuttles on this section of river. This is unfortunate, because the scenery within the CATIE canyon is superb, featuring hundreds of oropendolas, plus toucans and many blue morpho butterflies. It is still possible to run this section, but a long shuttle by road is now re-

**Rating Table: Reventazon at Angostura**

| Gage Height meters | Discharge cfs | cms |
|---|---|---|
| 1.0 | 1900 | 55 |
| 1.1 | 2100 | 60 |
| 1.2 | 2400 | 69 |
| 1.3 | 2650 | 75 |
| 1.4 | 3000 | 85 |
| 1.5 | 3300 | 93 |
| 1.8 | 4300 | 122 |
| 2.0 | 5100 | 145 |
| 2.2 | 5600 | 160 |
| 2.3 | 6400 | 180 |

Source: Instituto Costarricense de Electricidad reports.

quired. The old road into Peralta has been improved considerably, so this is now the preferred route for access to the Peralta section and for extended trips down the lower Reventazon.

A government-maintained gaging station is found right at the Angostura put-in, providing precise information about water levels. At standard discharge, the river runs approximately 1.5 to 1.65 meters on the staff gage. A level of 1.6 indicates a discharge of 3300 cfs (93 cms). At 2.0 meters, the river is pumping out over 4500 cfs (125 cms) and at 2.5 meters, a full 7000 cfs (200 cms). Running this section at levels above 2.0 meters is not recommended. Above that level, the holes become humongous and the eddies microscopic. Nonetheless, members of the U.S., Canadian, and Italian whitewater teams ran the Peralta section at a level of 3.0 meters during the winter of 1987. Two world champion paddlers ended up swimming and losing their boats when they attempted the left channel suicide run at Land of a Thousand Holes. Mere mortals would never have made it that far down the river at such a ridiculously high water level.

The water quality of the Reventazon is especially poor below the Rio Turrialba junction, so avoid ingesting water in this reach. Persons with open cuts should probably choose a cleaner river such as the Pacuare.

## Rio Reventazon

**Section:** Peralta to Siquirres (Pascua Section)
**Degree of Difficulty:** Class IV+
**Gradient:** 55 feet per mile (10.4 m/km)
**Length:** 16 miles (26 km)
**Put-in Elevation:** 1148 feet (350 m)
**Take-out Elevation:** 262 feet (80 m)
**Drainage Area:** 600 square miles (1540 km²)
**Average Discharge:** 4000 cfs (115 cms)
**Season:** All year; caution in rainy season

The Pascua section contains big, continuous Class IV whitewater with numerous play spots. Commercial trips put in three miles (5 km) further downstream at Bajo 52 Millas. There are a lot of pourover holes in the Pascua section, so it is preferable to paddle this section for the first time with someone who knows the river.

The second rapid of note below Bajo 52 Millas is found in a hard bend to the left. This is Mar del Norte (The North Sea) and it is full of big waves, big rocks, and big holes. The next named drop is Sacacorchos (Corkscrew). The name pretty much sums it up. After that is Campo Minado (Mine Field), another descriptive name for a rapid full of obstacles that should be avoided.

The meat of the Pascua section is a section known as Six in a Row. The six are Cola del Dragon (Dragon's Tail), The Wall, Frankenstein, El Horrendito (Little Horror), Surprise (Mente Sucia), and Aleta de Tiburon (Shark's Fin). El Horrendito is the biggest, most powerful rapid on the lower Reventazon. The river splits around a large island; the standard run is down the right branch. The island provides a convenient place to scout the rapid and its many holes.

# Río Pejibaye

**Section: Taos to Pejibaye**
**Degree of Difficulty:** Class III+
**Gradient:** 87 feet per mile

**Length:** 2.9 miles
**Put-in Elevation:** 2362 feet
**Take-out Elevation:** 2109 feet
**Drainage Area:** 49 square miles
**Average Discharge:** 805 cfs
**Season:** Wet season only: July through December

The upper Pejibaye (payhee BUY eh) is quite small but its relatively steep gradient and intimate character make paddling it worthwhile. Unfortunately, the severe floods of July 1987 temporarily rendered the Pejibaye unpaddleable, but the rapid rate of organic decay in the tropics will assure that the logjams are relatively short-lived. After a period of just two months, kayakers who know the river were able to run this stretch.

Local residents of Turrialba Roberto, Alvaro, Javier, and Santiago pioneered runs on the Pejibaye. First in inner tubes and later in a small raft, they made many trips down the river. During the low-water season, they snorkle the river at night to harpoon fish. With their detailed knowledge of every pool, riffle, and snag on the river, they now work as expert raft guides.

### Río Pejibaye

**Section: Pejibaye to junction with Reventazón**
**Degree of Difficulty:** Class II, III
**Gradient:** 40 feet per mile
**Length:** 4.4 miles
**Put-in Elevation:** 2109 feet
**Take-out Elevation:** 1935 feet
**Drainage Area:** 83 square miles
**Average Discharge:** 1185 cfs
**Season:** July through December, sometimes as late as February

When the upper section of the Reventazón is too high to consider a put-in at the powerhouse, the Pejibaye and Reventazón make a very nice combined run. As the river descends from the crest of the Talamanca

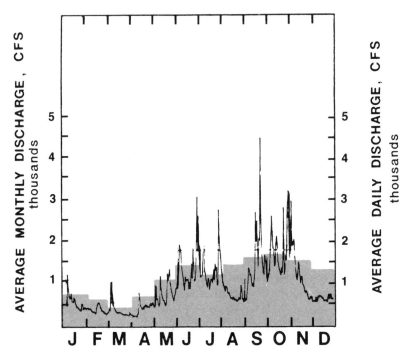

AVERAGE MONTHLY DISCHARGE, CFS
thousands

AVERAGE DAILY DISCHARGE, CFS
thousands

J F M A M J J A S O N D

Representative Hydrograph
Río Pejibaye

Range, it flows through a very scenic canyon and possesses excellent water quality. The river has a pool-drop arrangement of rapids, making it ideally suited for beginners and intermediate paddlers. As on all of the rivers in Costa Rica, it is very unusual to see another party on the Pejibaye, so you certainly won't have to worry about the sort of river crowding that has come to plague the Nantahala and the Youghiogheny.

Several logjams developed on this section of the river during the floods of July 1987, so use care in paddling this section for the first time. This section is very well-suited to beginning rafters, for it has easy rapids, clear water, and nice scenery. The lower Pejibaye makes a great warm-up run for the lower Reventazón, with its greater volume and more difficult rapids. This trip has become very popular with the cruise ship lines, which stop off at the nearby port of Limón.

# Miscellaneous Streams of the Caribbean Slope

The moisture-laden trade winds, which deliver such an abundance of water to the Reventazón and Pacuare, also produce dozens of other streams, which descend the steep slopes of the central cordillera and flow to the Caribbean Sea. Most of these other streams are quite small but are often very steep. Among these are the Sucio, Toro, Toro Amarillo, Tres Amigos, and the Peñas Blancas. Other streams of more than adequate slope and volume exist in the area but are inaccessible. Many first descents await the intrepid paddler who doesn't mind carrying his or her boat through miles of dense jungle.

These streams, more than any others in Costa Rica, are subject to sudden flash floods and substantial changes in channel characteristics as a result of frequent tumultuous floods. Paddlers should be on the lookout for flash-flood conditions, especially in the late afternoon, and should always be alert to the possibility of strainers.

## Río Peñas Blancas

**Section:** Poco Sol to San Isidro (bridge two miles from town)
**Degree of Difficulty:** Class IV+
**Gradient:** 115 feet per mile, 1 mile @ 214 feet per mile
**Length:** 4.0 miles
**Put-in Elevation:** 1246 feet
**Take-out Elevation:** 787 feet
**Drainage Area:** 43 square miles at put-in
**Average Discharge:** 587 cfs
**Season:** Wet season only

The Peñas Blancas (PAIN yas BLON cuss) is one of the recently discovered whitewater gems of Costa Rica's Caribbean slope. This incredible stream was not paddled until November of 1986, when a small

93

party led by the authors accomplished the first descent. The extreme gradient of the third mile led to considerable misgivings prior to the attempt, but with party members Bill Karls, Paul Mason, and George Strickland the group pressed on with some trepidation. What we discovered on that first run was not unrunnable waterfalls, but rather, some of the finest scenery and whitewater in the region.

Descending from the crest of the Cordillera de Tilarán, the Peñas Blancas ("white stones") drains an area of only 43 square miles above the upper gorge. In almost any other area of the world, such a tiny drainage basin would produce only a tiny creek, but this mountainous region receives over 200 inches of rain per year on its upper slopes, yielding a channel of more than adequate size, with abundant runoff. Because the stream drains a densely forested area including parts of the lush Monte Verde National Park, water quality is excellent.

The upper section of the Peñas Blancas flows through a dramatic gorge where the river has incised itself into the mountain escarpment. Below Poco Sol, there is little disturbance of the native jungle flora, and canyon walls rise to a height of over 700 feet. Dozens of sulfurous hot springs emerge from the young basaltic lavas and birds of spectacular plumage seem to infest every tree.

Access to the put-in at Poco Sol is from the south side of the river. A very rough dirt road leads from the small community of San José toward the put-in, although only four-wheel drive vehicles will be able to make it all the way to the put-in (see map). Most vehicles will have to stop about one-half mile short of the river, but the carry is made easier by the steep downhill approach. The put-in is beneath the hanging bridge.

One hundred yards past the put-in, the river swings hard left and drops through a steep drop that is severely constricted by large boulders. This one should most definitely be scouted, for it is the most difficult and dangerous rapid on the river, with several potent holes obstructing the direct route through it. This rapid is a marginal Class V, but it is the only one on the river. Unfortunately, it occurs immediately after the put-in and the paddler has no opportunity to warm up before entering it. This rapid has been named Tranquilo, Tranquilo—loosely translated, it means "take it easy." An easy portage could be made on the right.

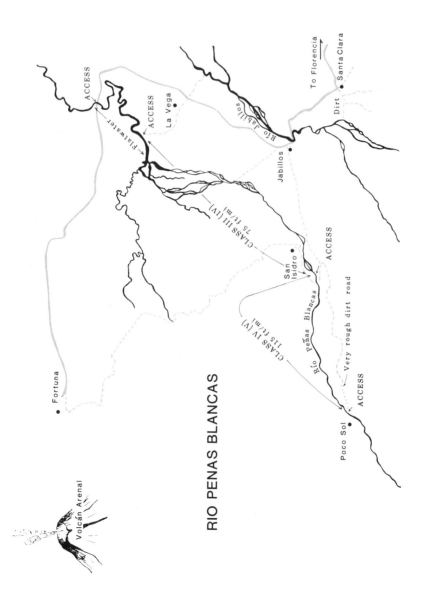

# RIO PEÑAS BLANCAS

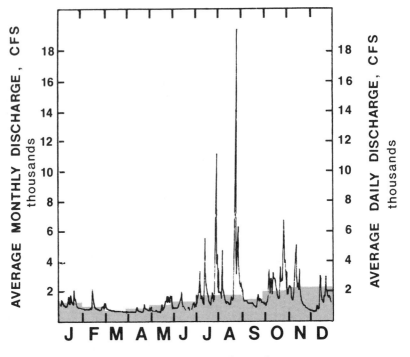

Representative Hydrograph
Río Peñas Blancas

For the next mile and one-half the river drops over numerous rapids of low, Class IV difficulty. All of them are straightforward and lend themselves to careful boat scouting. The fourth rapid in this sequence has a large pourover hole in it that should be easy to avoid, but as its name (Pablo y Miguel) suggests, a couple of us did not do so on the first descent. In the middle of this section is a rapid where the river swerves against the left wall and has succeeded in carving a large cavern in the cliff. One can eddy out in the middle of the rapid in a rock shelter that is at least 20 feet deep and 15 feet high.

As the river approaches a much narrower lower gorge, the gradient increases to 214 feet per mile for an entire mile. Such an extreme gradient often results in unrunnable rapids, but the Peñas Blancas accomplishes the descent in one long, continuous rapid. Spread out over a mile without a single pool, this 214-foot drop is only Class III+ in difficulty; it is a whitewater delight rather than a nightmare. We named this rapid Casado Especial. Its namesake is a traditional Costa Rican meal with rice, beans, meat, spaghetti, eggs, salad, potatoes, tortillas, etc. The rapid contains a similar quantity and variety of whitewater delights.

The last mile has a much lower gradient, but many fun rapids remain and the intervening pools provide an opportunity to enjoy the scenery and wildlife of the canyon. The high bridge outside of San Isidro marks the end of the canyon run of the Peñas Blancas. A steep trail leads to the road from the right bank.

As the deep, widely scoured floodplain suggests and the accompanying hydrograph confirms, the Peñas Blancas is prone to rapid increases in streamflow. The steep slopes of the headwaters gather the torrential rains that fall on the Cordillera de Tilarán very efficiently, sending them down the small tributaries and into the main canyon in very impressive volumes for a stream with a drainage basin of only 43 square miles. Great care must be taken, then, in deciding to run the upper canyon. No gage is available at or near the put-in, but one should be able to make an appraisal of flow conditions from the bridge at San Isidro. At runnable levels, the rapids below the bridge should appear runnable but scratchy. If the rapid downstream of the bridge indicates voluminous flows with large standing waves, the lower section would be a better bet. If the channel is continuous from bank to bank, head back to the Sarapiquí.


### Río Peñas Blancas

**Section: San Isidro to La Perla**
**Degree of Difficulty:** Class III+ (IV)
**Gradient:** 53 feet per mile, 4 miles @ 100 feet per mile
**Length:** 10.5 miles (7.4 miles to short take-out)
**Put-in Elevation:** 785 feet
**Take-out Elevation:** 230 feet
**Drainage Area:** 110 square miles at take-out

**Average Discharge:** 1400 cfs

**Season:** Rainy season only—July through September; occasionally thereafter until December

This lower section has an entirely different character from the upper section; the valley is much more open, the gradient is lower, and the river often splits into numerous channels. Thus, more water is required to run the lower section than the upper section, just the opposite of most rivers. Nonetheless, this section contains some very entertaining rapids and the scenery, though different, is still spectacular. On our initial trip down the river we saw a dozen or more ospreys, numerous oro pendulas, toucans, otters, and a crocodile.

Most of the rapids in this section are easily boat-scouted and have easily discerned routes. The primary exception is encountered about a mile below the put-in, just after the river splits into three channels and rejoins itself. This individual rapid is of low Class IV difficulty due to the contorted route that must be followed between jagged boulders and irregular holes. The sneak route is down the left side; the hero route is through the middle.

In the next few miles the river repeatedly splits into multiple channels, none of which carry enough water at normal levels to provide an entirely clean run. After six miles, the river reorganizes itself into a single channel. The upper take-out at La Vega is found another mile downstream and is highly recommended because the last four miles have very little gradient and no rapids. In addition, the bridge at La Perla has no convenient place to exit. A very difficult climb through dense vegetation is required there.

Throughout the lower section of the Peñas Blancas, the scenery is dominated by a panorama of volcanoes. To the west is Arenal, to the south is Poás, and to the southeast is the great Barva-Irazú-Turrialba massif. Arenal is quite active; it is not at all unusual to see spectacular steam-ash eruptions spewing from the crest. Arenal is the most impressive of the Costa Rican volcanoes, not because of its height (only 5356 feet), but because it rises dramatically from a base of only 1300 feet to its crest in a steep, symmetrical cone.

# Río Toro

**Section:** Valencia to Pital
**Degree of Difficulty:** Class IV+
**Gradient:** 88 feet per mile, 1.5 @ 125 feet per mile
**Length:** 7.4 miles
**Put-in Elevation:** 1280 feet
**Take-out Elevation:** 620 feet
**Drainage Area:** 60 square miles
**Average Discharge:** 750 cfs
**Season:** July through November

The Toro drains the northern slopes of Poás Volcano and flows parallel to the Sarapiquí. Indeed, the Toro has a great deal in common with the Sarapiquí; this upper section is nearly identical to the upper Sarapiquí in gradient, in difficulty, and in the character of its rapids.

The first two miles of the Toro are the steepest and the most remote. Rapids are tightly spaced and the stream flows through a small, heavily wooded gorge. The canyon walls are beautiful but it would be rather difficult to hike out from the first two miles of this section. Egress would certainly be easiest by hiking along the stream rather than by trying to climb the steep walls. Most of the upper rapids have long rocky approaches to steep endings. The upper sections of each rapid are wide open, but the lower parts require precise maneuvering to negotiate the rocky passages. No single rapid stands out in this section, but there are many drops of Class IV difficulty; the entire first half of this section contains non-stop pool-drop action.

In the lower half of the upper Toro the canyon opens up, farmland reaches the river banks, the gradient eases up, and the severity of the rapids decreases. Still, there are no flatwater stretches and the miles pass quickly. The take-out is at a bridge 1.7 miles east of Pital, a busy little farming community of approximately 1000 people.

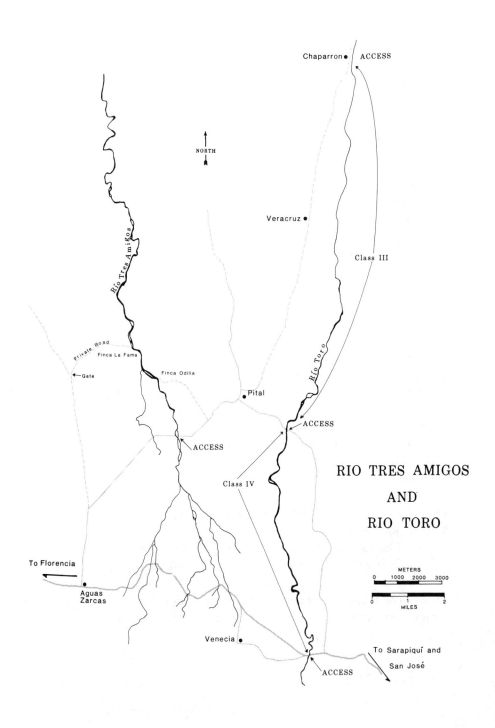

NORTH

Chaparron ● ACCESS

Veracruz ●

Class III

Río Tres Amigos

Río Toro

Private Road

Finca La Fama

Finca Odilia

← Gate

● Pital

← ACCESS

ACCESS

Class IV

RIO TRES AMIGOS

AND

RIO TORO

To Florencia

Aguas
Zarcas

METERS
0   1000  2000  3000

0        1        2
MILES

Venecia ●

To Sarapiquí and
San José

ACCESS

## Río Toro

**Section:** Pital to Chaparron
**Degree of Difficulty:** Class III
**Gradient:** 45 feet per mile, 5 miles @ 59 feet per mile
**Length:** 10 miles
**Put-in Elevation:** 620 feet
**Take-out Elevation:** 170 feet
**Drainage Area:** 74 square miles
**Average Discharge:** 940 cfs
**Season:** Wet season only—July through November most years

The lower section of the Toro is much less difficult than the upper, but like the upper, it is amazingly similar to the Sarapiquí. The river passes over innumerable boulder gardens and shoals, with many rapids crashing abruptly into steep walls at their termini. Like the lower Sarapiquí, this section of the Toro has spectacular tropical scenery and birds.

The take-out for this section is at a defunct footbridge at the village of Chaparron. The bridge is about one mile past a spectacular cliff above the river on the left bank. It is important not to miss the take-out because the road ends within another few miles; after that, the river courses through virgin jungles for 17 miles before joining the Sarapiquí. After another 6 miles the Sarapiquí joins the San Juan, which forms the border between Costa Rica and Nicaragua. The next possible take-out is another 33 miles down the San Juan to the Caribbean, then 68 miles down the coast to Puerto Limón!

# Río Tres Amigos

**Section:** Pital to Finca la Fama
**Degree of Difficulty:** Class II
**Gradient:** 38 feet per mile
**Length:** 3 miles
**Put-in Elevation:** 475 feet
**Take-out Elevation:** 360 feet

**Drainage Area:** Less than 50 square miles
**Season:** Wet season only—July through November

An intimate, tree-lined stream with clear water, attractive scenery, and abundant wildlife, the Tres Amigos is conveniently located between the Toro and the Peñas Blancas. If not for this proximity, it would probably never have been run due to its modest gradient and small size. The biggest drawback to attempting this run is the difficulty in finding a place to take out. The road to Finca la Fama is private, so unless you can convince the guard at the gate to break the rules and let your shuttle vehicle in, you will have to carry your boat out for almost a mile. The other option is to paddle just the first two miles and take out on the right at Finca Odilia. There are no convenient access points beyond Finca La Fama, although a very rough dirt road reaches the river another seven miles downstream at Gloria.

# Río Sucio

**Section: Junction with Río Hondura to Santa Clara**
**Degree of Difficulty:** Class IV+
**Gradient:** 137 feet per mile
**Length:** 6.0 miles
**Put-in Elevation:** 1575 feet
**Take-out Elevation:** 750 feet
**Drainage Area:** Approximately 75 square miles above put-in
**Average Discharge:** Approximately 1100 cfs
**Season:** All year

Dropping at breakneck pace off the northwestern flank of Irazu Volcano, the Sucio (SOO see oh) finally slows its rate of descent to a mere 137 feet per mile below the junction with the Hondura, as it leaves the Cordillera Central for the Santa Clara plains. In making this topographic transition, the river also changes from an unpaddleable series of cataracts to a non-stop series of Class IV rapids.

Scenery within the Sucio canyon is spectacular. The upper part of the

A typical unnamed rapid, Río Sucio. Photo by Rafael Gallo.

river flows through Braulio Carrillo National Park, where the riparian forest is incredibly lush. A full 84 percent of the park is still covered in virgin forest. Over 500 species of birds reside in or migrate through the park, including the magnificent quetzal, a bird with vivid blue, green, and red plumage and a tail that is longer than its torso. The high peaks of the Central Volcanic Cordillera can be seen up the gorge of the river and many waterfalls tumble down the canyon walls to join the Sucio.

The Río Sucio ("dirty river") gains its unique character and its name not from turbid channels draining hillside farms, but from iron oxide compounds leached out of the recent lava flows upstream. As a result, the river has a distinctively orange tint and a very bitter taste. In addition to the coloration and taste that it adds to the water, the iron compounds adhere to the rocks in the channel, giving them the texture of coarse sandpaper. This natural anti-slip compound makes scouting and portaging easier and safer, but it makes rafting impossible, for rafts cling to the rocks with great tenacity.

With its steep gradient, the Sucio provides constant whitewater action from the put-in to the take-out. The rapids are quite congested and very technical in nature. With its crooked course and steep drops, it is difficult to see very far downstream at any time. To complicate matters even further, there are few useful eddies in the upper section of the river. The Sucio should be avoided at even moderately high flows, for the larger drops become very pushy and the holes grow to the point that they become dangerous.

The larger drops are clean but complex; in most cases it is impossible to completely plan a route through them. Instead, one must be prepared to react quickly and improvise. A recent flood made two formerly innocuous rapids into the most difficult on the river. First comes Vortex, which is a very long, complex rapid. The trick here is to avoid three large boulders, each of which forms a grabby pourover hole. The most difficult rapid on the river is Perros Bravos—Beware of the Dogs—where two pourover boulders (the dogs) guard the entrance to a steep, congested drop. The difficult entrance sends the successful paddler into a ten-foot sluice that terminates in a shallow pourover hole. The far left route is possible as well, but only for those who are up to crashing a humongous hole at the bottom. The third of the more difficult rapids on the Sucio comes soon after a long, thin waterfall cascades into the river from the right. It is known appropriately as Boom-Boom. As the channel bends to the left, the river becomes quite congested. After a very difficult entrance, the rapid eases up somewhat for the remaining 100 yards of the rapid.

A distinct change in the character of the river occurs after four miles when the Río Patria joins from the left. The difference in appearance of the two streams is shocking; the Patria is perfectly clear, while the Sucio has the appearance of Tang. The Patria doubles the volume of water in the stream, widening the channel considerably and changing the nature of the rapids. The gradient of the river decreases here and the rapids become simpler and clearer, but the waves are much larger and the holes become much more powerful.

Toward the end of the run, the river changes character again, taking on a tendency to split into multiple channels. As many as six different channels coexist in places, and these channels are regularly reworked by

Take-out on the Sucio. Photo by Rafael Gallo.

floodwaters roaring down from the mountains. The Sucio actually splits below the take-out into two main channels, the Sucio and the Chirripó. The Chirripó flows directly to the Caribbean, while the Sucio joins the Sarapiquí, which in turn joins the San Juan.

At normal flows, the Sucio is at the same time technically demanding and pushy; many of the holes are distressingly grabby. At high water levels, the character of the river is quite different. Although it becomes very pushy and continuous, the holes are much more passive. As long as you remain in control, a high-water run on the Sucio is fun, fun, fun.

# Río Toro Amarillo

**Section: End of Calle Los Angeles to highway bridge at Guapiles**
**Degree of Difficulty:** Class IV

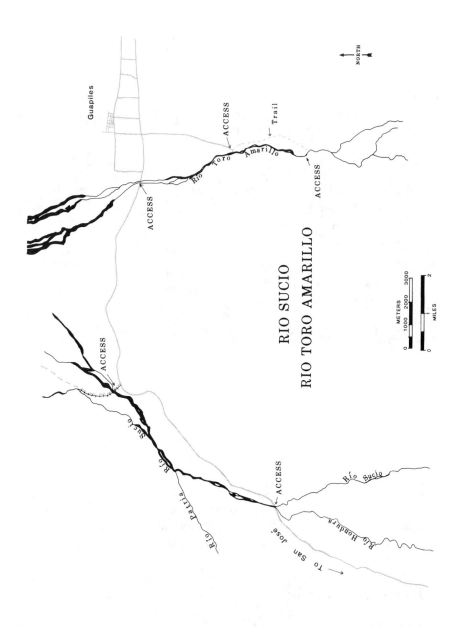

RIO SUCIO
RIO TORO AMARILLO

**Gradient:** 131 feet per mile
**Length:** 3.0 miles
**Put-in Elevation:** 1380 feet
**Take-out Elevation:** 980 feet
**Drainage Area:** 53 square miles
**Average Discharge:** 600 cfs
**Season:** June through December

This short section of river is quite similar in character to its sister river, the Toro. It is a boulder-bed river, with most rapids consisting of irregular rocky shoals. Like the Toro, the Toro Amarillo (TOR oh am uh REE oh) is a raging bull at times of flood, leaving behind a wide bouldery course whose low-water channel is quite congested and steep. There are many places for a boat to pin in these rapids; quick, decisive maneuvering is a must.

The short duration of the accessible, paddleable whitewater on the Toro Amarillo make it an unlikely candidate for a primary destination, but its proximity to the Sucio and the easy shuttle make it a good second run. With the new San José–Guapiles highway, it is possible to leave San José in the morning, paddle the Sucio and Toro Amarillo, and return to San José in time for dinner. Few rivers in Costa Rica offer such convenience of access.

# Río Corobici System

What is a stream system with an overall gradient of eight feet per mile doing in a whitewater guidebook? It is included primarily because of its spectacular scenery and wildlife, although it does have a surprising number of rapids for its gentle gradient. These streams flow through an area of Guanacaste that lies just outside of the Caballero Wildlife Reserve and Palo Verde National Park. These lands contain many of the same features and biologic wonders that the parks were designed to recognize and preserve. Migratory ducks, ibis, caracara, and wood storks are common. Howler monkeys rattle the canopy of trees with their bloodcurdling cries, while iguanas lounge in the trees and Jesus Christ lizards put on their famous show on the river's surface.

Guanacaste experiences a dramatically dry period from November until May, but the streams of the Corobici system remain paddleable throughout this period due to the diversion of the waters of the Arenal River into the Magdalena, which flows into the Corobici, which in turn joins the Tenorio. A massive hydroelectric/irrigation project has dammed the Arenal and sent its waters through a four-mile-long tunnel under the continental divide. The power generation and irrigation schedules insure adequate flows for boating throughout the year, except on Sundays, when electrical demands are low. The river corridors form a verdant oasis in the midst of the seasonal aridity of Guanacaste, thus attracting wildlife in incredible concentrations. Huge trees reach out across the stream channels from both sides of the river, encompassing the streams in welcome shelter from the desiccating Guanacaste sun. The abundance of water, shelter, and fish makes this area a virtual aviary.

## Río Magdalena/Río Corobici

**Section: Sandillal to Corobici**
**Degree of Difficulty:** Class II, III
**Gradient:** 19 feet per mile

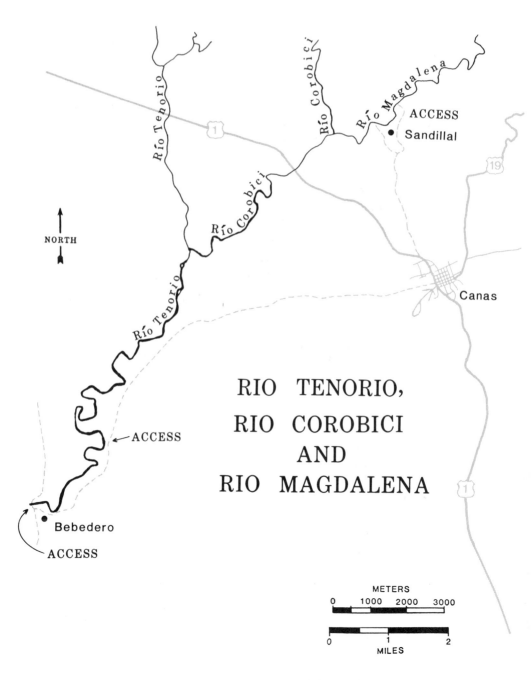

NORTH

ACCESS
Sandillal

ACCESS

Canas

ACCESS

Bebedero

ACCESS

RIO TENORIO,
RIO COROBICI
AND
RIO MAGDALENA

METERS
0   1000   2000   3000

0        1        2
MILES

Río Corobici System   109

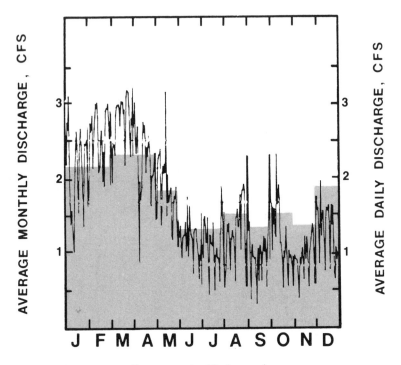

Representative Hydrograph
Río Corobici

**Length:** 2.6 miles
**Put-in Elevation:** 164 feet
**Take-out Elevation:** 115 feet
**Drainage Area:** 123 square miles (plus a large area from the Atlantic slope)
**Average Discharge:** 1800 cfs
**Season:** All year

This is a moderately large river flowing through a small creek bed. As a result, the channel is filled to its banks with clear, fast-moving water. Most of the river channel is open and clear, but in places it is split into multiple channels by huge boulders. These boulders have a tendency to pick up strainers, so great care should be taken in avoiding them. Eddies are hardly to be found in this entire reach of the river and the few that are available are very squirrelly.

About a mile and a half down the river, the Corobici (core oh bee SEE) joins from the right, as the river drops over a three-step rock shelf on the left. Eddy out behind the large tree on the left and take the opportunity to examine the hand-constructed basins, which the Corobici Indians used to catch fish and wash their clothes in. This is also an excellent place to swim and observe wildlife.

The last stretch of the river above the bridge at Corobici is a long straightaway where trees are draped over the river. Boat-billed herons are found in large numbers here, flying from tree to tree. Just above the bridge is a Class III rapid. The entrance is against the left bank, so great care must be taken to stay out of the bankside bushes and shrubs. The favored route is toward the center of the river, where a nice surfing wave lies.

A short section of the Magdalena above the aforementioned put-in has been paddled. It contains Class IV whitewater but its narrow course is extremely congested with strainers, and eddies are altogether absent. It is not recommended.

### Río Corobici/Río Tenorio

**Section: Corobici to Bebedero**
**Degree of Difficulty:** Class I, II
**Gradient:** 8 feet per mile, 3 @ 15 feet per mile
**Length:** 13.2 miles
**Put-in Elevation:** 115 feet
**Take-out Elevation:** 15 feet
**Drainage Area:** 123 square miles
**Average Discharge:** 1800 cfs
**Season:** All year

The scenery and the wildlife along the lower Corobici are legendary. At the nearby Palo Verde National Park, over 300 species of birds have been sighted and most of them can be seen along the Corobici as well. Among the more commonly seen birds are ospreys; mot-mots; blue, silver-throated, and boat-billed herons; jacanas; kingfishers; crested caracaras; and cormorants. Howler monkeys, iguanas, and many other varieties of lizards are also common. After the first bend in the river, there are no signs of civilization for over eight miles; the riparian forest and its wildlife dominate the landscape.

During the first third of this section of the Corobici, the current moves quite rapidly and the river divides repeatedly around small islands. Strainers develop regularly in these narrow channels, so use caution in choosing a route, especially in entering blind curves. Class II rapids are common but eddies are difficult to find—it is important to remember that this is a very small stream to which the waters of the larger Arenal have been added. This greatly augmented flow fills the channel to the brim, leaving few still places in the channel.

At this point, the Tenorio joins from the right. Although the Corobici provides the majority of the flow, the river is known as the Tenorio from this point on. In the second third of this section, the Tenorio maintains its high velocity but there are few rapids. The reduction in whitewater intensity is more than compensated for by the increase in abundance of wildlife, however. Watch for armadillos and caramoundi in addition to the species listed above. Overhead, monkeys leap from tree to tree and iguanas hang lazily from the branches.

As the river approaches tidewater in the lower third of its course, its velocity is greatly diminished and even reverses itself on incoming tides. The channel meanders frequently and civilization once again begins to encroach on the waterway.

# Río Chirripó del Atlantico

Originating high on the eastern flank of Cerro Chirripó, Costa Rica's highest peak, the Chirripó del Atlantico flows through some of the most isolated, pristine alpine and subalpine terrain in all of the Americas. No roads approach the stream until it has flowed for over 40 miles and dropped 10,000 feet from the crest of the Talamanca range. During that descent, it picks up numerous tributaries, which often join the deep canyon of the Atlantico by dropping over dramatic waterfalls. The stream is accessible only at two points within its canyon, where primitive trails lead to a few isolated dwellings and small farms.

### Río Chirripó Atlantico

**Section: Chirripó Abajo to Playa Hermosa**
**Degree of Difficulty:** Class V, VI
**Gradient:** 84 feet per mile, up to 170 feet per mile
**Length:** 18 miles
**Put-in Elevation:** 1770 feet
**Take-out Elevation:** 260 feet
**Drainage Area:** 311 square miles
**Average Discharge:** 3640 cfs
**Season:** June through January

The Chirripó del Atlantico remained an unpaddled mystery until quite recently. From the topographic maps it showed great promise: virgin rainforest without farms, houses, or people for almost 20 miles, a steep gradient, and incredible mountain scenery. Flowing parallel to the Pacuare and only eight to ten miles from it in places, it was correctly assumed that the Atlantico contained incredible scenery, challenging whitewater, and excellent water quality.

Several parties planned first descents on the Atlantico in 1984, but it was a small group of kayakers from Rios Tropicales outfitters that made the first run in December of that year. December is ordinarily a month of greatly diminished rainfall throughout Costa Rica, but conditions were unusually wet that year. When Tom Wise, Rafael Gallo, Earl Alderson, and Jim Reed began the six-mile hike to the river from the end of the road, they found hip-deep mud and very difficult walking conditions on the trail. It took the group an afternoon and the following morning to reach the river, with heavy rain falling intermittently. During their night on the trail, they found shelter in a small barn.

The initial elation of the group on finding the first two miles of the river to contain exhilarating Class IV whitewater was soon tempered by the harsh reality of endless Class V and VI rapids and rapidly rising water levels. There is no way to exit the canyon except to continue downstream, and each roaring tributary added to the woes of the exploratory run. During the second day on the river, the group was able to cover only two kilometers because most of the reach was unrunnable and portages were extremely difficult in the narrow boulder-studded gorge. On the third day, the group was eventually forced to run a Class VI nightmare that they dubbed The Gauntlet when no feasible portage route could be found.

Out of food and exhausted from the constant portages and difficult rapids, the group finally reached the mouth of the Río Moravia. The Moravia joins the Atlantico by dropping 1000 feet from Laguna Moravia in only 1.6 miles, producing a spectacular chain of waterfalls. Below the mouth of the Moravia, the gradient of the Atlantico drops to 55 feet per mile and the rapids diminish in difficulty in a nice progression from Class V to IV, to III, and finally to Class II. A very primitive dirt road leads to Playa Hermosa, but it is probably easier to paddle another eight miles to the paved road at Bristol.

Two other groups paddled the Atlantico in early 1987, at much lower water levels. One group found ideal water levels for an expert wilderness expedition but the other group did not have sufficient water to make the trip at all enjoyable. Both groups found it necessary to make a number of portages even at low water levels. It is very hard to find that ideal water level between the frustration of insufficient flows and the fear and very real danger produced by high flows on the Atlantico. In addition, the river is susceptible to rapid rises due to the heavy rainfall that occurs on the windward slopes of the Talamanca range.

We do not recommend the Chirripó del Atlantico. Despite its beautiful mountain scenery, challenging rapids, clear water, and splendid isolation, the difficulties and hazards associated with running this river are simply too great.

# Valle de Talamanca, Valle de Estrella

Between the massive Talamanca range and the Caribbean Sea is a profusion of streams, which drop from the rain-drenched windward slopes of the Talamancas to the sea. With rainfall of over 200 inches per year, these streams carry tremendous amounts of water to the Atlantic, maintaining substantial flows even during the dry spring months.

The entire region is sparsely populated, remaining the domain of the native Indians. No roads penetrate the vast jungles and even the trails are extremely hard to follow. As a result, rivers such as the Coen, Lari, Uren, Estrella, and Telire remain largely unexplored. The opportunities in this region are nearly limitless, but lack of access has stopped all but two short attempts.

In February of 1986, a small group of kayakers attempted the Telire. Jim Reed, Jim Elliott, and Rafael Gallo started at the end of the road at Suretka, with the intention of going 15 to 20 miles upstream. They hired four local Indians with mules to carry their boats and guide them through the jungle to their desired put-in area. After a half-day of travel, the Indians with the mules quit and returned to town, having found the trail too tight for the boats on the pack animals. The group continued for another day with their guides. At that point the trail was so narrow and treacherous that the remaining guides gave up, so the group continued upstream for another full day by paddling up the pools and portaging the rapids. After two and a half days of exhausting work, they had travelled about 12 miles upstream and decided to head back downstream.

The verdant jungle in this area is probably the largest expanse of virgin tropical rainforest in all of Central America. It is at the same time overwhelmingly beautiful and intimidating in its vastness; while admiring the incredible vegetation, wildlife, and sheer wilderness, the group could not escape the feeling that they were trespassing in no-man's-land.

Finally paddling downstream, the kayakers returned to Suretka in just five hours. At this low water level, the Telire flows through a very broad channel of flood-deposited boulders and gravel, with Class III rapids in a pool-drop arrangement. One Class V+ rapid was portaged. High discharge conditions of June through November would probably render the trails impassable and the rapids unrunnable. Entering the broad Valle de Talamanca, the Telire bifurcates frequently. In this last section, the river splits into as many as ten separate channels, only to rejoin and eventually form the mighty Sixaola.

# Recommended Reading

For more information on any aspect of the history, geology, climate, or natural history of Costa Rica, we recommend the following:

## Books

*Costa Rica: A Country Study*, edited by Harold D. Nelson. Washington, D.C.: U.S. Government Printing Office, 1983.

Part of the Army's area handbook series, this volume provides a comprehensive overview of the history, political system, culture, and geography of Costa Rica.

*Costa Rica: A Geographical Interpretation in Historical Perspective*, by Carolyn Hall. Boulder, Colorado: Westview Press, 1985.

Although written in a somewhat technical format and style for an academic audience, this book yields a wealth of information about Costa Rica and provides many insights into its society.

*The National Parks of Costa Rica*, by Mario A. Boza and Rolando Mendoza. San José, Costa Rica: INCAFO, 1981.

This book provides a fascinating introduction to the national parks by means of some very interesting text and excellent color photography. A profile of each park's history, geology, and ecology is included.

*Costa Rican Natural History*, edited by Daniel H. Janzen. Chicago: University of Chicago Press, 1983.

The definitive guide to the flora and fauna of Costa Rica. Academically oriented but richly illustrated and quite interesting to those without advanced training in tropical botany or zoology.

# Periodicals

"Costa Rica Steers The Middle Course," *National Geographic*, July 1981.

Typical *National Geographic* material: great photographs, and a nice mix of human and natural history. Just the thing to convince a skeptical spouse that the trip is not only safe, but essential.

"Safe Adventuring in Central America: Rafting Costa Rica's Río Pacuare River," *River Runner*, Jan.-Feb. 1984.

Slim Ray's short article provides an enticing glimpse of one of Costa Rica's great rivers. The photographs tell it all.

"Hollowdogs & Hollowed Logs: At Play in the Land of Pura Vida," *Canoe*, April 1984.

An imaginative approach to describing the joys and wonders of the General and Pacuare. Author Paul Hoobyar focuses on surfing at The Whirlpool and Chachalaca.

"Costa Rica, The Twig Syndrome, and The World Records that Got Away," *Outside*, December 1986.

While the subject of this article is fishing in Costa Rica, it is most definitely applicable to paddling. Wherever the author mentions fishing, substitute kayaking. Whenever he describes burnout as a sport-fishing guide, raft guides will immediately know just what he means.

"Gringos Find Big Fun on Central America's Ultimate Play River," *River Runner*, September 1986.

# Index

## About the Authors

### Michael W. Mayfield

A native of North Carolina, Michael now lives in Boone, where he is an assistant professor in the Department of Geography at Appalachian State University. He is married and is the father of three wonderfully active children. His academic interests in fluvial geomorphology and hydrology are easily pursued on the nearby Watauga, Doe, and Nolichucky rivers.

### Rafael E. Gallo

Rafael was born in Ithaca, New York, but soon moved to El Salvador, where he spent his childhood. He became active in kayaking while attending the University of Tennessee and has paddled extensively across the United States, Central America, and in Europe. Rafael is now president and co-owner of Rios Tropicales, a whitewater rafting and kayaking outfitter in San José, Costa Rica.